THE 10 ESSENTIALS OF FOREX TRADING

THE 10 ESSENTIALS OF FOREX TRADING

The Rules for Turning Patterns into Profit

Jared F. Martinez

McGraw-Hill

New York   Chicago   San Francisco   Lisbon   London
Madrid   Mexico City   Milan   New Delhi
San Juan   Seoul   Singapore
Sydney   Toronto

5 6 7 8 9 0   FGR/FGR   0 9 8

ISBN-13: 978-0-07-147688-1
ISBN-10: 0-07-147688-1

This publication is designed to provide accurate and authoritative information in regard to the subject matter covered. It is sold with the understanding that neither the author nor the publisher is engaged in rendering legal, accounting, or other professional service. If legal advice or other expert assistance is required, the services of a competent professional person should be sought.

> *—From a Declaration of Principles jointly adopted by a Committee of the American Bar Association and a Committee of Publishers.*

McGraw-Hill books are available at special quantity discounts to use as premiums and sales promotions, or for use in corporate training programs. For more information, please write to the Director of Special Sales, McGraw-Hill Professional, Two Penn Plaza, New York, NY 10121-2298. Or contact your local bookstore.

This book is printed on acid-free paper.

Library of Congress Cataloging-in-Publication Data

Martinez, Jared.
  The 10 essentials of Forex trading / by Jared Matinez.
    p. cm.
  ISBN 0-07-147688-1 (alk. paper)
  1. Foreign exchange futures.   2. Foreign exchange market.   3. Speculation.
I. Title.   II. Title: Ten essentials of Forex trading.
HG3853.M37 2007
332.4'5–dc22

                                            2006036400

Dedication

I T IS WITH THE utmost respect and my sincere admiration that I dedicate this book to my wife Susan; who has helped me watch my thoughts as they became my words, helped me watch my words as they became my actions, helped me watch my actions as they became my habits, helped me watch my habits as they became my character, and most importantly helped me build my character, which ultimately protected our destiny. She is my partner for life!

I further dedicate it to our eight children and three grand children, who have been a miracle in my life and forced me to stay humble. Thank you for being the grinding stone in my life . . . some days you really ground me down, but most days, you really polished me up allowing, me to shine.

May you all enjoy each day of your life—I love you all!

Acknowledgments

WITHOUT ANY WARNING to NASA, President Kennedy announced to the world in 1961 that within the decade, America would send a man to the moon and safely bring him home. After his speech, the leaders of NASA frantically called the White House declaring his proclamation to be impossible. A clear message was sent back to NASA from the White House stating: "Nothing is impossible."

The White House was right!

My wife Susan, has been my "White House" and our eight children; Tania, Sonya, Jared, Jacob, Isaac, Rachael, Joshua and Jordan, and our three grandchildren; Jeffery, Deanna and Nadia, have been her joint "Chiefs of Staff" supporting her as she delivered her consistant message to me: "keep going—nothing is impossible!"

I further wish to thank *adversity*. Had it not been for the countless people who mustered up the courage to face adversity, the world would have never heard their "pearls of wisdom." It is with my sincere gratitude that I bring tribute and give credit to all the authors from whom I have borrowed their "pearls of wisdom." Their pearls of wisdom, acquired from their personal moments of adversity, became my strength as I fought my own adversities.

Next on my list, I wish to thank three key business people that have heavily participated in my emotional and financial success: Isaac Martinez, Jacob Martinez, and Riana 'van den Berg' Rawson. They are MTI's key strategic Vice Presidents and have been dedicated in putting MTI on the worldwide map. It is their talent and capability that allowed me the freedom to write this book.

I would like to give special thanks to Riana "Martinez" Rawson (who truly belongs in my family) and whose unconditional support for me, my wife, my family and business made this book possible. Her sheer genius never ceases to amaze me.

Next, I wish to thank all the MTI clients worldwide for having faith and trust in me. Thank you for opening up your homes and your hearts to me and my family. It has been through your perception of the world, the market and your countless challenging questions that have allowed me to widen my perception of the world and the market.

In addition, I would like to thank all our staff and worldwide partners at MTI for their dedication, support and belief in our vision. You are not only great business partners, but have become some of my best friends. I want to give special thanks to the founding members of our MTI team: Jonathan Schneider, Pedro De Sousa, Jeff Todd, Mauricio Passaro, Rob Rawson, Frank Josenhans, Sam Sego, Rick Purifoy, Nickie Hube, Rachael Martinez, Ricard Mouton, Kevin McGowan, Dennis Du Plessis, Cassie Van Wyk and Hector Ruiz.

I am deeply grateful to Jeanne Glasser and all the staff at McGraw-Hill who have participated in bringing this book to market. Thank you for believing in me.

I cannot finish my acknowledgements without recognizing my parents who constantly grounded me in an attempt to harness my adventurous spirit. A special thanks to my two moms: my real mom for constantly telling me, "You always need to do what's right because you were meant to achieve great things in life," and my mother-in-law "whom I call mom" for being there during one of our most challenging times - thank you for your support and positive attitude!

I give tribute to you all!

Contents

Dedication   v

Acknowledgments   vii

Introduction   xv

1   So You Want to Trade FOREX?   1

Two Wolves   1

Follow the Rules   4

Your Personal Litmus Test   5

Your Life's Purpose   14

Conclusion   15

2   Introduction to the FOREX   17

History of the Forex Market: How It All Began   19

What Is the FOREX?   21

Types of Traders   22

How Do Traders Get Paid?   23

Bulls and Bears   25

Types of Orders   25

The Market Traders Institute Philosophy   28

The Three levels of Trading   28

The Reality of Trading   29

The 21-day, 3 Percent Rule   29

Conclusion   30

3   Self-Empowerment via Trading Software   31

How to Determine Market Direction   35

Using Indicators to Determine an Entry Point   37

Using Indicators to Determine Exit Strategies   41

Using Multiple Time Frames to Trade   44

Conclusion   44

4   Trading Japanese Candlesticks   47

The History of Japanese Candlesticks   47

How to Read a Japanese Candlestick   49

Reading a Japanese Candlestick Chart   50

How to Find a High   50

Understanding the Different Japanese Candlesticks   52

Candlestick Formations   56

Bullish Candlestick Formations or Buy Signals   57

Bearish Candlestick Formation or Sell Signals   62

Trading Candlestick Patterns   68

Conclusion   70

5   The Financial Game of Support and Resistance   71

The Game   73

How do Bulls and Bears Score Points?   74

Identifying Highs and Lows   75

Resistance and Support   75

Learning to Short the Market   81

Past Resistance can Become Future Support   83

Past Support can Become Future Resistance   84

Visually Observing the Game   84

Conclusion   86

6   Trends and Trendlines   89

A Trend Is Your Friend   89

Trading a Trend Until it Bends   91

Spotting an Uptrend   96

Drawing Uptrend Lines   97

Finding and Drawing Inner, Outer, and Long-term Uptrend Lines   98

Incorrect Ways of Drawing Uptrend Lines   100

Finding and Drawing Downtrend Lines   105

Finding and Drawing Inner, Outer, and Long-term Downtrend Lines   106

Incorrect Ways of Drawing Downtrend Lines   107

Trends Inside of Trends   109

Trading Channels   110

The Value of Trend Lines   111

Conclusion   111

7   Buy and Sell Zones   113

Trends   115

Buy and Sell Zones   117

The Sell Zone   117

Shorting the Market When It Enters the Sell Zone   121

The Buy Zone   122

Going Long in the Market When It Enters the Buy Zone   126

Conclusion   126

8   The Fibonacci Secret   129

The History of Fibonacci   131

The Fibonacci Numerical Sequence   132

The Fibonacci Sequence in Nature   132

The Fibonacci Retracement and Extension Ratio Relationship   140

The Value of Adding the Fibonacci Numbers to your toolbox   146

Conclusion   147

9   The Reality of the Fibonacci Secret   151

Fibonacci Market Movement on September 11, 2001   151

Fibonacci Retracements Everywhere   155

Conclusion   158

10   Fundamental Analysis   161

Fundamental Announcements Analysis   161

Trading Days Versus Trending Days   167

Increased Risk with Trading Fundamental Announcements   168

World Economies   170

The Importance of Fundamental Announcements   171

Conclusion   174

**11   Consolidating, Bracketing, Accumulation,
          or Sideways Movement   175**

Consolidation Factors   176

Strategy 1   178

Strategy 2   181

Not All Fundamental Announcements Move the Market   182

Strategy 3   183

Bull and Bear Traps   184

Conclusion   185

12   Learning the Rules of Equity Management   187

What Is Equity Management?   187

The Equity Management Formula   193

Risk versus Reward   195

Percentages Mean Nothing When Trading   195

Conclusion   197

13   The Final Analysis   201

Education First   204

Our Habits Control Our Lives   205

Finding Your Pot of Gold   205

Glossary   209

Index   213

Introduction

I AM THRILLED TO BE a part of your trader's journey and I am excited about your interest in Forex. Forex, or the *for*eign *ex*change market, offers incredible financial opportunity for those who are ready for the adventure, but it can be disastrous and financially devastating for those who are unprepared. My focus as an author is to be a mentor to those readers eager to enter the world of Forex trading. Some of the material in this book took me years to discover, develop, and just plain figure out.

I hope you will realize that this book, although written primarily for traders, is ultimately about self-improvement. I have discovered that no one can become successful at trading, or for that matter at anything, without first establishing their personal constitution. It is this aspect of yourself that either destroys you or allows you to succeed in life, and that includes Forex.

To be successful in your financial journey, you will need to be prepared for what the market demands the most—*change* and *discipline*! If you cannot find the courage to change and then remain disciplined to that change, you will be unable to develop a trading strategy that aligns with your personality and your perception of life.

Every trader is looking for the "holy grail"; that little piece of truthful and accurate information that works consistently! In my own trader's journey, I discovered that the holy grail is knowing *when to get in the market and why* and *when to get out and why*. If you can learn the *when* and the *why*, you will be able to make market movements work for you allowing you to capture the majority of potential profit from the move. When you do this, you have discovered your personal holy grail in trading! I believe this book can become your holy grail if you let it!

Trading needs to be fun, emotionally exciting, personally and financially fulfilling, and stress-free. If you are going to be successful at trading, you will need to acquire a trading strategy that is easy to execute, easy to understand, easy to obey, and that works for you consistently. You will also need to master your emotions. Success lies in mastering four skills, three of them technical. These technical skills include knowing:

1. How to find *market direction* in any time frame, anytime, 24 hours a day.

2. How to establish a successful *entry strategy* that works consistently. Every trader wants the market to move in his or her direction from entry.

3. How to create two solid *exit strategies*: one to protect yourself financially should the market not go your way, and one to capture profit if it does.

The remaining skill is more difficult; it is learning how to overcome the battle that takes place in your mind. Believe it or not, our daily destructive habits hold us back from achieving what is rightfully ours in this life. Learning to become a successful currency trader is a dream highly sought after by countless people around the world. I am here to tell you that it is a worthy and attainable dream.

I have learned that achieving one's goals and dreams is a matter of mental discipline. Dreams are attainable! However, there is a set of steps that needs to be mastered in order to make your dreams come true. This book will help you to learn these steps and to acquire the courage and commitment to take them. Always remember that man was not created to just get by—he was created to reach his highest potential!

> *"If another person can do it, YOU can do it!"*
> —*My mom*

1

SO YOU WANT TO TRADE FOREX?

TWO WOLVES

One evening, a very wise, old Indian chief was speaking with his grand-son about life, telling him about the internal battle that goes on inside all people.

He said, "My son, inside all of us there exists a constant battle between two wolves. One wolf is very evil. It forces you to deal with anger, envy, jealousy, sorrow, regret, greed, arrogance, self-pity, guilt, resentment, inferiority, lies, false pride, superiority, and a self-centered, destructive ego. The other wolf is good. It helps you to experience joy, peace, love, hope, serenity, humility, kindness, benevolence, empathy, generosity, truth, compassion, faith, self-respect, and to develop a giving, constructive ego."

The grandson thought about it for a minute and then asked his grand-father, "Which wolf wins?"

The wise, old Indian chief replied, "My son, the one you feed."

*   *   *

Thousands of books on investing and wealth accumulation have been written and hundreds of seminars created to help individuals reach their financial goals. These materials are created by professionals whose guidance enables individuals to improve their financial performance and who provide productive techniques that can potentially create wealth. Regardless of all the available material designed to improve one's financial status, one fact remains for certain: *Successful people will do what unsuccessful people won't or can't do!*

There are successful people who have either been taught by a mentor, acquired some special knowledge, or implemented disciplines that enabled them to achieve their financial goals. The saddest part about this process is that most people do not display the sufficient humility and open-mindedness to acquire all this information and mentorship at an early stage in their lives.

I am adamant about one thing: if you are on the hunt for success in any field or any walk of life and have not yet acquired it, then perhaps you have been looking in the wrong places. I have traveled the world and interacted with many different cultures, and I've learned through this experience that there is a clear reason why people are not successful at what they attempt to do. The reason is universal: successful people focus on feeding the good wolf.

Individuals who manage their mediocrity or poverty in life are focused on feeding the wrong wolf—the evil wolf. They carry around past emotional baggage and, in time, it becomes so heavy that all they can think about is survival. This mindset seriously affects their personality, performance, and ability to maintain emotional control, which is essential for success in life and success in trading.

I have noticed a pattern among people around the world, regardless of country, race, or culture; they become what I call *rainbow chasers*. Every few months they come up with a get-rich-quick plan, but these endeavors are doomed to fail, and then comes the inevitable blaming. Very seldom do those people accept responsibility for their outcome and look inside themselves to discover why they have failed. They go from one business opportunity to another, never achieving their end result, and are clearly locked into self-destructive habits. They repeat their bad habits, continue to chase rainbows, and fail at just about everything they do.

Life is not capricious; it will always provide the rich and poor alike with new opportunities. Forex is such an opportunity. This book will help you understand how to trade in Forex, or the *for*eign *ex*change market, and reap the financial outcome you desire. Please embrace this inform-ation with excitement, because you will be given the exact education and trading tools used by some of the best money managers in the world. Whether you succeed or fail is solely determined by what is in your head and your heart.

Many traders who fail tend to blame the market or other external factors. It is everyone else's fault but theirs. Believe it or not, this is how history repeats itself in their lives. If this describes you, then this book can really help you make a change in your life. Not only does it teach the technical side of trading, but also it will force you to address some of those unproductive bad habits.

When trading Forex, your daily actions will be based on a clear productive mindset of:

Reappointment versus disappointment
Resilience versus resentment
Better versus bitter
A winner not a whiner
A star not a scar
A victor not a victim
A conquerer not a crumbler

The reality in life is that the choice is yours. Bad things happen to everyone, and you won't be spared as you learn to trade Forex. Your success will be determined by how confident you feel, what you think, and how you respond when bad things do happen. In any financial or business endeavor, success starts in your head, is fueled by your heart, and the results are driven by your actions. These will determine your Forex experience. In this book, you will learn certain disciplines and habits that will help you become a better trader.

There are three questions you have to ask yourself before you trade:

1.   Do I want to make a lot of money?
2.   Do I want to make an average income?
3.   Do I just want to get by and break even?

You need to understand these things about yourself because the market tends to be self-fulfilling. Remember, you will always find what you are looking for, whether it be good or bad.

Nothing in life is perfect, and if you set yourself up with an unrealistic expectation that things should be perfect, you put yourself in a position to focus only on negative events. If you bring this perspective to the trading table, it will have a similarly destructive effect. Uncover who you are and what you are looking for before you trade so that you can lay the proper foundation on which to build your trading career.

FOLLOW THE RULES

The first step to successful trading is to analyze your character to ensure you are not bringing your bad habits to the trading table. Your moral constitution, work ethic, and personal beliefs will mirror your trading habits. If you are a rule breaker, then there is no point in trying to learn a new successful skill that requires rules to be followed. If it is in your character to break rules, then learning a new successful skill that can change your financial future is useless. You will simply break the rules and self-destruct.

I know a person who is habitually late to work. Despite the fact that his employer requires him to arrive on time, he doesn't seem to believe that showing up on time is that important, which is why he has had to change jobs four times in the past year.

As a result of his tardiness, he is repeatedly terminated. Yet he refuses to change his behavior. He is more willing to go through the trouble of searching for a new job than he is to change a simple, yet critical, destructive personal habit. What I find with most unsuccessful people is that they fail to see the importance of following rules that will lead to their success, such as showing up on time. The truth is, changing little unproductive habits makes a huge difference to one's success.

People underestimate how important preparation is for success. However, the reason they get locked into poverty and mediocrity—only getting by—is that they show up to the battlefield totally unprepared and unprotected. Their focus quickly turns from the cause they were fighting for to survival and self-preservation. "I didn't bring the proper armor to fight this war, I didn't think I'd be here this long, I don't have enough food to survive, I don't have enough ammunition," and so forth. With that survival mentality, one's attitude turns from that of a conquerer to that of a crumbler.

To survive the coming learning curve and successfully transition to a productive career trading on Forex, you will need to properly arm yourself. Creating your personal constitution is like acquiring the best helmet possible to protect your most important asset—your mind. Your mind is the epicenter of your body and the control tower of your destiny.

You first need to identify, and perhaps define, who you truly are. The following exercise will help you discover your personal constitution. Once you have completed this exercise, you will be able to see what you need to change in your personal life to become a successful trader. This exercise is what I call a *litmus test.* (A Litmus test commonly refers to a test done to determine substance.) Taking this personal litmus test forces you to face the brutal reality of whether you are made of "gold" or "fools' gold."

YOUR PERSONAL LITMUS TEST

1. *Are you more honest than dishonest?* Do you always tell the truth? or do you exaggerate and make up stuff along the way? As a child, I acquired the habit of exaggerating from my dad. He would exaggerate about nearly everything he did, saw, and experienced. Yet when I challenged him about his falsehoods, his justification was that "exaggerations make the story more interesting."

    Not surprisingly, I began to follow in his footsteps. When I began dating my wife, she challenged me about my exaggerations the same way I did my dad. When we were alone, she would calmly say to me, "That didn't happen that way. When you exaggerate, you are outright lying. That is not a good habit!"

    Telling the truth is critical. It builds relationships and earns security, trust, and respect from those with whom you associate. It helps others know who you truly are. It also prevents future trading missteps.

    After you have been taught how to trade, if you are in the habit of exaggerating, you'll begin to lie to yourself and others about your success. You will lie to yourself about how well you follow the rules when in reality you are trading on emotion and hunches. And if you lie about your level of success, that bad habit will curse you when everyone wants to see proof of your trading prowess. They'll want to know your secrets of supposed success. Be honest in everything you do!

2. *Are you a promise keeper or a promise breaker?* Integrity is all about making sure your word equals your deed. If your word does not equal your deed, then you are a promise breaker. No one likes a promise breaker. You will not be able to attract the right people in your life unless you become a promise keeper.

    When you make commitments to yourself and others, you need to keep them. If you are not a promise keeper, you will bring this bad habit to the trading table and you will not follow the rules as you trade. You will make promises to yourself and then break them. Believe me when I say that if you promise never to trade without a protective stop-loss order, which is an order that protects you from losing all your money in a single trade, and then break that promise, your career as a trader will quickly be over. Avoid this fate—be a promise keeper.

3. *Are you a rule maker or a rule breaker?* Freedom is something of a paradox because in order to be free, you must abide by a plethora of rules. Just look at all the rules when driving your car. But the more you obey the rules, the safer you are when driving. Breaking the rules, however, will endanger your life and may cost you your freedom.

   Our lives are filled with rules. From an early childhood we learn our parents' household rules. Then we learn rules about school, about dating, about working, about marriage, parenting, and so on. The rules in our life protect us and help us get where we are going faster and safer. Breaking those rules creates risks, problems, and, eventually, setbacks. These setbacks can take you completely off track and dramatically delay you from achieving your goal in a timely manner.

   Learning to trade, and being successful at it, requires that you follow certain rules. Ignoring the rules will cause you trouble when you are trading. You will be driven by your emotions and will be caught up in chasing the market, changing your mind, and breaking every rule in the book in the spirit of trying to save yourself. Don't get yourself caught in this position.

4. *Are you a good or bad listener?* Being a good listener has its rewards. The greatest reward comes to those who develop the art of hearing what is *not* said.

   I used to be a bad listener, constantly interrupting people when they were talking and completing their sentences for them. I assumed I already knew what they were going to say and where they were going with the conversation. And yet I was almost always wrong. To overcome this habit, I had to learn to keep my mouth shut until the person speaking to me finished what they were saying.

   Interrupting someone's conversation can potentially get the topic off track and plunge all involved into confusion. Imagine the impact of such an interruption on a trade in process. Learning to be a successful trader requires good listening skills. You may ask, "What am I listening to?" You are listening to the market's story.

As the market moves, it "tells" a story. Because history repeats itself, where the market has been begins to predict where it is going. If you interrupt its story and try to second guess what it is going to say, you will set yourself up to make a poor decision. Although trading charts are unable to express themselves verbally, they do communicate to traders who are good listeners. You cannot find success in trading by disrupting the flow of the market's conversation. Listen, don't interrupt.

5. *Do you think before you speak or speak before you think?* Have you ever wished you could take back something you just said? Your comments and words are like ringing a bell; once the bell is rung, you cannot "un-ring" it! Your words are like the sound of the bell—they resonate! People who speak before they think are often branded as ignorant and annoying; few are respected. On the other hand, we respect and look up to people who think before they speak; we value their conversation and opinions because they are carefully considered.

Which do you do? Are you habitually putting your foot in your mouth? Or do you respond with educated answers and arguments? As a trader, you must engage in a conversation with the market and your response can either be ignorant or intelligent. If you are disciplined enough to think before you speak, you will probably find success in trading. However, if you insist on speaking before you think, the market will allow you to prove your ignorance.

6. *Do you think before you act or act before you think?* The conscious and subconscious parts of your mind are your greatest assets and your greatest liabilities. The conscious mind dissects, considers, and categorizes everything you see and hear. If action is needed, the conscious mind thinks through how it will execute the action. If action is taken, the subconscious mind records the thought with the action and matches the two for future reference. In the future, all we have to do is think that thought, and the subconscious mind stands by to automatically execute the exact action that matched the thought. That is how a habit is formed.

Think about it once, do it once, and you have started a habit. Think about it three times, do it three times, and you now have established an automatic habit—good or bad. When you create good or bad actions, your subconscious mind takes over automatically, enabling you to do things without thinking. That is both good news and bad news.

If you are involved in any unproductive actions that have turned into bad habits, you are unconsciously incompetent. That is when your mind is working on destructive autopilot and you need to regain control. You need to become conscious again in order to recognize your bad habits and admit they are not benefiting you. When you recognize your bad habits, you are able to learn a new skill or a new habit to replace the unproductive one. Learning a new, productive skill or habit is the first step to managing your success.

When you learn a new skill, you usually have to think through each step of the action. Thinking through that action and successfully executing it is called *conscious competence*. When you are disciplined enough to consciously repeat it when the situation requires, your subconscious mind automatically replaces the previously recorded action associated with the thought and forms a new habit. The subconscious mind does not think, it just recalls and executes the actions that matched the thought. The more you repeat the action—good or bad—the more that habit becomes unconsciously automatic. If you are locked into executing bad habits, you are *unconsciously incompetent*. If you are locked into executing good habits, you are called *unconsciously competent*. The road to success involves the recognition of *unconscious incompetence*, then passing through to *conscious incompetence*, working your way to *conscious competence*, and eventually arriving at *unconscious competence*. In achieving this you have purged yourself of your bad habits and have replaced them with productive, automatic, good habits that allow you to perform successful actions without thinking about them. It is like learning to drive a car.

Think back: the first time you got into the driver's seat, you literally had to think through everything that needed to be done just to pull out of the driveway. That process took about 15 minutes because you had to consciously think through everything you did. You were consciously competent. Now, if you began to drive and received speeding tickets and got into accidents, you became unconsciously incompetent. It was when you consciously committed yourself to stop speeding and to look in every direction to avoid accidents that you became a consciously competent driver. Today, if you have been driving and are free from speeding tickets and accidents, you are considered an unconsciously competent driver. You have now become unconsciously competent in your successful driving habits. You probably take about three seconds to pull out of the driveway, probably driving part of the way with your knee as you juggle a cup of coffee in one hand and a cell phone in the other, focusing on the conversation rather than each individual skill needed to drive the car. Can you see how powerful your mind is and how critically important it is to properly think through everything before you act?

When it is time to trade, you must think before you act. If you act before you think and make mistakes, your subconscious mind will take over and record all your ignorant actions and subconsciously create bad trading habits. That is how you start to lose money or just get by in trading. Successful traders think before they act to execute successful trading habits.

Failure is like cancer. You don't treat cancer by cutting it out. If you have to remove the cancer, much of the time it is too late. You treat cancer by preventing it and you treat success by creating good habits from the beginning. This way you are preventing failure. As you learn to trade, you will need to get in the habit of thinking through all the details potentially involved with that trade. You will need to have checklists that cover all the details. You will need to get in the habit of creating a trading plan and maintaining the discipline of trading your plan. That habit forces you to think before you act, avoiding impulsive, emotional actions that generate unsuccessful trades. The market has no remorse for ignorance and impulsive action. The ignorant will suffer. Think before you act.

7. *Do you manage your emotions or do your emotions manage you?*
    Most financially successful people are very unemotional when it comes to business decisions. Believe it or not, successful business is nothing more than making and executing unemotional decisions that make economic sense. It is no different than unemotionally figuring out a mathematical equation. Two plus two will always equal four, regardless of how desperately you wanted it to be five—it will always equal four.

    Unsuccessful business is nothing more than making and executing emotional decisions that don't make economic sense. For example, holding onto unproductive employees because you like them, does not make economic sense and is a bad business decision rooted in emotion.

In life, there are good emotions and bad emotions. The bad
emotions usually don't serve us well, whereas the good emotions
enhance our lives. When it comes to business, you need to make all
your decisions unemotionally. Your decision process needs to be
educated, logical, and unemotional. Any financial decision made in
the heat of negative emotion will hurt you much more than it will
ever help you.

When it is time to trade, the more you rely on your emotions to
make your decisions, the more money you will lose. The more you
rely on your education and logic, the more money you will make.
Thinking through problems unemotionally allows you to stay
focused on achieving long-term happiness and success. Bad things
happen to all of us, and many times we have no control over them.
The reality is that we have no control over the cards we are dealt, we
only have control over what we do with those cards. What we do
have control over is how we handle the situation—emotionally or
unemotionally. Successful traders manage their emotions; unsuccessful traders let their emotions manage them.

8. *Are you responsive or reactive?* When something doesn't go according to plan or doesn't go your way, do you throw a temper tantrum
and have a "mental meltdown"? Unsuccessful people usually do.
Successful and positive-thinking people are able to process properly
the negative things that happen to them, put them into perspective,
and move on. If your emotions control you, you are going to be
more reactive than responsive and you will probably go through life
with unhappiness, poverty, and mediocrity. As a rule, just about
everything negative that happens to us is either self-inflicted or the
result of not paying attention to red flags, warnings signs, or details.
Accepting responsibility for our own actions is such a painful event
that we find it easier to react and blame someone else rather than
analyzing what really happened and responding by creating a system to avoid that situation again.

If you bring your reactive bad habits to the trading table, the market will know exactly which emotional buttons to push. When it
does, you will run like a scared rabbit being pursued by a pack of
hungry wolves. Running scared is not conducive to calming down
and thinking through your next move. Reacting versus calmly
thinking through the situation and responding eliminates your
ability to see clearly what happened. When it comes to any crisis,
in trading or otherwise, you owe it to yourself to respond logically,

not emotionally. Reactive trading will cause you to lose all your money, whereas responsive trading will allow you to think through your next move and take advantage of the next opportunity that knocks.

9. *Is your ego more constructive or destructive?* Are you more humble or more arrogant? Do you make your decisions based on your pride and ego or based on logic regardless of the consequences to your ego? If you go through life allowing your decisions and actions to come from a destructive ego, you will be no different than the person who purchased a brand new sailboat and ignored the first line of the owner's manual: "Avoid storms at all costs. Do not go looking for storms as you sail your boat, they will naturally find you!" A destructive ego is nothing more than a storm chaser living through one bad storm after another. A constructive ego keeps you focused on all the details necessary to avoid any and all storms as you sail through life.

A person with a constructive ego believes their mind is like a parachute; it only works when it is open. A person with a destructive ego thinks he or she already knows everything. Unfortunately, when it comes to trading, the market will teach that destructive ego the true definition of humility. When conflict shows its face to a constructive ego, the constructive ego, through humility, will in the end fight to be happy rather than right.

10. *Are you more positive about life or more negative?* How you answer this question will greatly determine your overall happiness in life. Is your glass always half empty or half full? There is a law that is every bit as much valid as the law of gravity: it is called the law of attraction.

The law of attraction stipulates that whatever we think about, those thoughts will radiate out of our being and create circumstances and events and attract people that align with our thoughts. When we think positive thoughts, that positive mindset will radiate out of us, creating positive circumstances and positive events in our life and, as a result, will attract positive people into our lives. The flip side of this law is also true. When we think negative thoughts, that negative mindset will create negative circumstances and negative events in our lives, attracting negative people into our lives.

The power of this law plays an incredible part in determining your success or failure in life. Positive people are considered optimistic people, whereas negative people are considered pessimistic, but the only real difference between an optimist and a pessimist is that the optimist believes there is an answer to every question and a solution to every problem, whereas the pessimist believes most questions have no answer and most problems are unsolvable. This mindset significantly limits the pessimist's potential, success, and happiness in life. Optimists, on the other hand, create positive outcomes via the law of attraction.

The simple shifting of your mindset from negative to positive changes your entire world. Negative people are constantly shifting blame and frustrated about how unfair life is; they walk around with a victim mentality. Positive people accept responsibility for their circumstances and place themselves in a position to figure out how to avoid negative situations in the future.

If you want to become a successful trader, you will have to purge your negative attitude and adopt a positive mindset and attitude. Negativity when trading only creates more negative circumstances, more negative events and financial losses.

11. *Do you fear your mistakes or do you embrace them and learn from them?* All people make mistakes, but only wise people learn from them. The only true mistake is the one from which we learn nothing. Mistakes show us what needs improvement. Without mistakes, how would we know what we need to work on?

Avoiding situations in which you might make a mistake could be the biggest mistake of all. When you have the courage to go out on a limb and make a decision, right or wrong, you risk making a mistake. Everyone makes mistakes. Strong people make as many mistakes as weak people—the difference is that strong people admit their mistakes, laugh at them, learn from them, and become stronger. When you make mistakes, problems usually surface, which creates fear and anxiety.

Pessimists live a life fearful of making any mistake because that mistake will create a problem, and just about all problems, in their opinion, have no solution. Optimists can make just as many mistakes as, if not more than, pessimists. However, when a problem arises for an optimist, they aggressively work on it, believing it can be resolved, and the second they see the solution, the fear and anxiety dissipates.

When life hands you lemons, do you waste time sucking on them or do you learn to make lemonade? Making mistakes is part of being human. Just about all of life's important lessons can only be learned the hard way, usually by making a mistake. Mistakes can be resolved and corrected as long as you believe there is a solution. So when you make a mistake that creates a problem, you need to muster the courage to face the problem head-on until a solution is achieved. As you do this repeatedly, unemotionally, you will develop the skill of effective problem solving. Remember, failure is not the problem; the problem lies in the time we waste lamenting over the problem rather than focusing in on the solution to the problem. Failure is not falling down; failure is staying down.

Learning from your mistakes is critical to your success. Choosing not to learn from your mistakes as you learn to trade will cause you to become a repeat offender. Your subconscious mind will take over and will form an unproductive bad habit, costing you money. You must pay attention to your mistakes and embrace them with a positive attitude.

12. *Do you focus on what you have or on what you have lost?* As you go through life making mistakes, you will inevitably lose things along the way—money, close relationships, personal property, you name it. But how much time do you spend holding onto those mistakes? How much time do you spend calculating your losses and wishing you had back everything you had lost? The longer you dwell on past failures and losses, the longer you will stay captive in your current state of failure. You must let go of your past failures and focus on where you are going.

Have you ever wondered why the rearview mirror is 50 times smaller than the windshield? The windshield is so much larger to help us stay focused on where we are going versus where we have been. Holding onto past wounds or losses will only stand in the way of achieving your rightful success as a trader. Every trader loses money and makes money as they trade, but successful traders will make more money than they lose. Successful traders spend no time worrying or thinking about their losses; they stay focused on the next opportunity that is knocking.

People that manage their poverty or mediocrity are so busy holding onto their past that they can't grab onto future opportunities. Holding onto past losses or failures creates a bitter mindset. If you come to the trading table with a bitter mindset or victim mentality, you will bring with you all your past emotional baggage that has stood in the way of you becoming successful at anything you attempted in the past. It will stand in the way of you becoming a successful trader. If you want to be successful at trading, you must focus on what you have gained versus what you have lost.

13.   *Are you a goal setter or a goal quitter?* When you set out to do something, do you persist until you succeed or do you get discouraged and quit along the way? One of the most important habits to develop is the habit of finishing what you started. My son recently graduated from high school. At his graduation ceremony, the principal stood up and congratulated everyone for completing 12 years of education. He also pointed out that during the last year of school, 48 percent of the students in the graduating class had dropped out. They came so close, but they did not persist until the very end.

Most people in life are rainbow chasers; they set new goals almost daily. Most of the time their new goals have nothing to do with yesterday's, last week's, or even last month's goals. As a result, they never move forward in any one direction. You need to believe there is a reward at the end of every journey you embark on, a "pot of gold" at the end of each rainbow, or you will give up and never achieve your goal.

Setting goals helps you create a road map in life, outlining where you are going. Without that road map you can easily get off track without even knowing it and not know how to get back on. If you do not create goals as you learn to trade, you will not have any recognizable milestones of achievement.

Any great achievement will be accompanied by setbacks, but beginning with a clear goal in mind will keep you on track to reach your goals even after you hit a detour. Traders who set goals and persist until they succeed reach their pot of gold at the end of the rainbow. A trader's pot of gold is described as executing your trades correctly 100 percent of the time. That does not mean you will make money 100 percent of the time, rather, that you consistently make more money than you lose. Persisting to achieve your realistic goals is nothing more than discipline in action.

YOUR LIFE'S PURPOSE

Successful people live by what they believe not by how they feel. They are what I call constitution-based versus feeling-based. Successful people have strong convictions. They are very clear about their personal constitution and their purpose in life. Constitution-based people will do whatever it takes to do the right thing, because it aligns with who they are. They have their priorities in check and have the right perspective and attitude when it comes to facing the internal battle between the two wolves that exists in all of us. Your personal constitution will mirror your trading results.

CONCLUSION

Take the time to answer honestly the previous constitution-based questions to allow you to build a solid foundation for your long-term success in trading. You have an obligation to your personal future, happiness, health, family, and income to establish a solid personal constitution.

Developing a solid personal and trading constitution is the *first step* of your journey toward successful trading on Forex. I started this book on trading by pointing out the importance of creating an emotional and psychological constitution before teaching you any technical skills. What good does it do to teach you technical skills if you do not have the courage to execute them? Why teach you trading rules if you are a rule breaker? There is no point to teaching you how to take advantage of new trading opportunities if you cannot let go of your past mistakes and failures.

Developing a solid personal and trading constitution will be the *first step* of your journey toward finding your rightful pot of gold in trading. I look forward to accompanying you on your journey to the end of your trading rainbow. Let our journey begin.... .

2

INTRODUCTION TO THE FOREX

I WILL NEVER FORGET one trip to Australia, back in early 2001. I was working out of our office in Sydney, preparing for a class, when I was e-mailed the list of attendees. The registrar told me there were 26 Australians signed up for the class and one Scotsman, named Ian, who had a very strong Scottish accent.

The next morning I started class the way I always do, asking everyone their names, their current occupations, why they want to learn trading on the Forex, and, more importantly, why they chose to get involved with my company, Market Traders Institute, versus another.

We started going around the room introducing ourselves and eventually came to Ian. Ian was an older fellow, perhaps in his late fifties, and in great physical shape. "Hel-ow chief," he said in an extremely strong Scottish accent. "My name is Ian, and I am from Scotland. I just happened to be here in Australia for a bit when your advertisements caught my interest. I called your office and they told me all about you, so I came here because I was told you could teach me how to trade on the Forex and make money. Is that true?"

I confidently answered, "I will do my best, Ian."

He said, "That's not what I asked. Now pay attention to the question. Can you teach me how to trade on the Forex and make money?"

A bit more warily, I responded, "I can inform you all about the Forex and I am willing to share everything I know, but it will be up to you to learn, understand, and properly implement all this information with the discipline I will teach you."

He said, "Okay, that's a fair statement." Then he said, "Chief, I am a mercenary by profession. Do you know what that is?"

"Ian, I have learned never to assume anything. The term 'mercenary' here in Australia could be different, so why don't you inform the class what you mean."

I was absolutely not prepared for what he said next. "Chief, I kill people for foreign governments, and I am here to tell you *that if this is a scam and if you can't teach me how to trade on the Forex . . . I will kill you.*"

There is nothing worse than being caught off-guard or put on the spot in front of a crowd. Everyone's eyes in the class were now focused on me. So I threw my hands up in the air and said, "Wow, no pressure, Ian." Then I looked at the class and said, "Class, I know we have only scheduled three days of training, but we may be here for a month because I am going to go over each and every single detail I know about the Forex. This will be the best class I have ever given, and, rest assured, if I don't know the answer to a question, I will go to the ends of the earth to answer it before I leave Australia, because I don't want to have to look over my shoulder the rest of my life wondering if Ian is near." The class burst into loud laughter.

The best way to learn something and remember it is to teach it to someone else, so after I teach a concept for about 45 minutes, I instruct the class to teach each other. I have the person on the right teach the concept to the person on their left, and after they are done I have the person on the left teach the concept to the person on their right. Little did I realize this teaching technique would potentially save my life.

When I divided the class into pairs that day, I believe God protected me by having an odd number of students. When I got to Ian, I said, "Ian, I will be your partner." Although some of the other students asked to partner with me, I told them, "Nothing personal, but my life is at stake here, so I am going to work with Ian." Thankfully, they all understood.

Looking back, I must say that was one of the most detailed, and perhaps one of the best, classes I have ever given. Every time someone had a question, I immediately asked, "Ian did you understand the question?" Then I would follow up with, "Ian, did you understand the answer?" If he said yes,

I would make him explain it to me and the rest of the class as an insurance policy against my life. I am happy to report that both Ian and I are still alive. In fact, Ian is now an active client of ours and has taught me a lot in return.

Two of the greatest things he taught me were how to perform under pressure and, more importantly, how to keep things simple with respect to teaching Forex trading. For example, at one point, Ian could only recognize and understand uptrends. "I can't see or understand downtrends, Crown reversals, consolidations, Gartleys, or harmonic vibrations," he told me, "but I sure can see an uptrend." A simple fact about trading on the Forex is there are six major world currencies traded against the U.S. dollar; when three go up, the other three go down. They have to move in opposite directions to keep the world economy in balance. So when the currency of Ian's choice stops trending up and begins to reverse and trend down, Ian goes and finds one of the other three currencies that have reversed from a downtrend and are now trending up. He keeps his trading simple.

As I move forward teaching you about the Forex, I will do my best to explain the concepts in this book as if you are "Ian" and that my life is dependent on providing you with the most accurate and detailed information to help you get started.

HISTORY OF THE FOREX MARKET: HOW IT ALL BEGAN

BRETTON-WOODS ACCORD

The modern Forex market was established around 1973. But the Bretton-Woods Accord of 1944, which was established to stabilize the global economy after World War II, is generally accepted as the original beginning of the foreign exchange market. It created the concept of trading currencies against each other and the International Monetary Fund (IMF). Currencies from around the world were fixed to the U.S. dollar, which in turn was fixed to gold prices in hopes of bringing stability to global Forex events. All currencies were allowed to fluctuate around that value but only within a narrow trading range. Central banks agreed to intervene in the event that their country's currency moved or threatened to move outside that trading range. If the fixed value of a country's currency shifted outside that trading range, that country had the right under the articles of the agreement to declare that a fundamental imbalance is in existence. As a result of this fundamental imbalance, it created a revaluation or devaluation of the country's currency.

In 1971, the accord finally failed, however, it did manage to stabilize major economies of the world, including those of America, Europe, and Asia.

FREE-FLOATING CURRENCIES

In late 1971 and 1972, two more attempts were made to establish free-floating currencies against the U.S. dollar: the Smithsonian Agreement and the European Joint Float. To "float" a currency simply means to create a policy by which a strong economic currency is used, such as the U.S. dollar (USD), which in turn is anchored to the price of gold as a benchmark (also known as the *gold standard*) to bring stability to a volatile global economic situation. All other weaker economic currencies are then fixed against the USD and allowed to fluctuate, or float, no more than 1 percent on either side of the fixed rate. If the fixed rate moved more than 1 percent, the central bank of that country was required to intervene in the market until the exchange rate was brought back to within the 1 percent band.

The Smithsonian Agreement and the European Joint Float agreement were similar to the Bretton-Woods Accord but allowed a greater range of fluctuation in the currency values and widened the band in which currencies were allowed to trade.

The Smithsonian Agreement was just a modification of the Bretton-Woods Accord, with allowances for greater fluctuation, whereas the European Agreement aimed to reduce the dependence of European currencies on the U.S. dollar. But after the failure of the three agreements, nations were allowed to peg their currencies to "freely float," eventually being mandated to do so in 1978 by the IMF. The free-floating system managed to continue for several years after the mandate, yet many countries with weaker currency values incurred major economic devaluation against certain countries that had stronger currency values.

EUROPEAN MONETARY SYSTEM

European currencies were among those most affected by the strength of the U.S. dollar and the British pound (GBP). In July 1978, the European Monetary System was created to counter its dependence on the USD. But by 1993, it was clear that this European Monetary System had failed. Shortly thereafter, retail currency trading opportunities as we know them today started to be enjoyed by smaller investors willing to take similar risks as that of banks and large financial institutions.

DEVALUATION

By the late 1990s, stability issues arose in Europe, and major financial problems erupted in Asia. In 1997, there was a major currency crisis in Southeast Asia, which forced many of the countries' economic currencies to float. The devaluation of currencies continued in the Asian currency markets, and confidence in trading the open Asian Forex markets began to fail. However, countries with stable currencies, and the concept of trading currencies, remained unchanged.

THE INTRODUCTION OF THE EURO

By this point, the Europeans were already very comfortable with the concept of Forex trading, but the rest of the world was still unfamiliar. The establishment of the European Union in 1992 gave birth to the euro seven years later in 1999. The euro was the first single currency used as legal tender for the member states of the European Union and became the first currency to rival the historical leaders—the United States, Great Britain, and Japan—in the foreign exchange market by providing financial stability that Europe and the Forex market had long desired.

WHAT IS THE FOREX?

Forex is an acronym for *for*eign *ex*change, a market where people exchange the currency of one country for the currency of another in order to do business internationally. Typical situations in which such currency exchange is necessary include payments of import and export purchases and the sale of goods or services between countries. Forex is also called the *cash market* or *spot interbank market*. The *spot market* means trading on-the-spot, at whatever the price is at that moment.

Prior to 1994, the Forex retail interbank market for small individual speculative investors or traders was not available. A *speculative investor*, or *speculative trader*, is one who looks to make a profit on price movement in the market and is not looking to hold onto any currency long-term. But with the average minimum transaction size of $1,000,000, smaller traders were all but excluded from participation in this market. Then in the late 1990s, retail market maker brokers (companies that facilitate the trades for speculative traders) were allowed to break up the large interbank units and offered individual traders the opportunity to participate in the Forex market as we know it today.

Forex is considered the largest financial market in the world. The term *market* refers to a place where buyers and sellers are brought together to execute trading transactions. More than $1.5 trillion U.S. dollar is traded daily on the Forex. By comparison, $300 billion dollars is traded daily on the U.S. Treasury bond market and $100 billion dollars is traded daily on the U.S. stock market, for a total of $400 billion dollars per day. Forex trades nearly four times that volume daily, exceeding the daily combined activity of all the other financial markets.

Forex has no physical location—transactions are placed via the Internet or telephone—but is composed of approximately 4,500 international world banks and retail brokers. Individual traders wanting to profit by speculating on price changes can only access this market through a Forex broker, such as I-TradeFX.com. It is a good practice of a speculative trader to only deal with Forex brokers that are regulated by the governmental bodies in their respective countries.

TYPES OF TRADERS

Trading currencies involves the fluctuation of one currency in relation to another. That is the main difference between trading currencies and stock trading—you always have to deal with two instruments, or currency pairs, whereas in stock trading you only deal with one instrument. The definition of a currency pair, or currency cross, is trading one currency for another currency, and you need a currency pair to execute a trade on the Forex. Speculative currency trading, just like speculative stock trading, involves exchanging one currency for another *in anticipation of* a price change in your favor.

There are two types of traders on the Forex: consumer traders and speculative traders. A consumer trader wants long-term ownership and is not as concerned with daily price movements, whereas a speculative trader is *only* concerned with daily price movement, as that is where the profit potential is. Speculative traders are also called *scalpers*—they are trying to scalp a profit in a small price movement. Long-term position traders enter the market and stay in for a week, a month, or years. Short-term, or day traders, will enter the market for 5 minutes, 30 minutes, or even 4 hours, and then exit, but they are usually in and out within a 24-hour period.

Although brokers will assure you that Forex trading is commission-free, it is important that you understand there still *are* costs involved. That cost is called the *spread*, which is what you will be charged to get access to the Forex market. The spread is the difference between the *buy price* and the *sell price* of a specific currency.

Envision attending an auction where there are several buyers for a particular item. The auctioneer hopes to sell the item for $10.00 and has asked for bids. One bidder offers $4.00. The difference between the $4.00 bid and $10.00 asking price is $6.00, which is called the spread. As bidding gets closer to the asking price, the spread tightens up. When the bidding gets to $9.95, there is a $0.05 spread, and when the bidders agrees to buy it for $10.00 and the seller agrees to sell it, you have a transaction. There are spreads between all currency pairs that are traded, and they average 3 to 6 price interest points, or *pips*, on the major world currencies (which are considered to be the U.S. dollar [USD], the British pound [GBP], the Japanese yen [JPY], the European euro [EUR], and the Swiss franc [CHF]). The value of a pip averages about $10.00. Currencies from small countries are called off-brand currencies and can have spreads as much as 500 to 1,000 pips. The broker retains the spread, which is the difference between the buy and the sell price. This is done when a trader enters a trade and upon execution of the trade the spread, should the trade not go your way, is deducted from the trader's account. Example: If the sell price is 4 pips lower, or $40.00 less, than the buy price, and you buy a currency and immediately go to sell it without any movement in your favor, you would lose $40.00, or 4 pips. To break even, the market would need to move up 4 pips in your direction. To make a profit, the market would need to move more than 4 pips in your direction.

HOW DO TRADERS GET PAID?

Price interest points, commonly known as *pips*, are usually expressed in decimals. Depending on the pair of currencies being traded, pips are usually the last numbers of the decimal. As shown in the EUR/USD example of Figure 2-1, pips are measured when the fourth digit after the decimal point moves up or down.

A trader's financial reward is measured in pips, which are then converted into dollars. Most traders on the Forex trade with what is called *leverage*. This is borrowing or using a broker's money to trade. You acquire leverage by posting a bond or a deposit with a Forex broker who then allows you to trade using the broker's money. When a trader executes a trade on the Forex, the trader is buying or selling currency in units referred to as *lots* (which is a set quantity of money). There are typically two types of lots that traders will trade. A $100,000 unit is called a regular lot, and a

FIGURE 2-1   EUR/USD (One Hour Chart) Time Versus Price

$10,000 unit is called a mini-lot. When you buy and sell a regular lot, you get paid $10.00 a pip versus $1.00 a pip on the mini-lot.

For example, if we were buying or exchanging one currency lot on the EUR/USD currency pair at the exchange rate of USD $1.28 for every 1 euro, or 1.2800 price point (see Figure 2-1), we would enter the market at that point. You will see that the currency moved in our favor to 1.2840, at which point we decided to exit the market, selling our lot for a profit of 40 pips. To equate the 40 pips with money value, remember the following: 1 pip = approximately $10.00 on a $100,000 transaction or $1.00 on a mini-lot transaction. If we made 40 pips in profit on this transaction, we would have made 40 pips × $10.00 = $400.00 on a $100,000 account or 40 pips × $1.00 = $40.00 on a $10,000 account.

The average minimum deposit for trading with leverage is 1 percent, which means that for every $100,000 lot you trade, you must have $1,000.00 in your margin trading account. For mini-lots, you will need a minimum of $100.00 in your margin trading account on deposit.

Trading can be a worthy full-time profession or a great way to earn secondary income. Either way, you will need to learn the three basic skills of trading as you watch price movement against time.

The three critical skills you must learn are

1.   How to determine the current trend on any time frame
2.   How to develop an entry strategy that works consistently
3.   How to develop an exit strategy that works consistently

Once you master these three skills, you will be in a position to take advantage of the significant profit potential in this market.

BULLS AND BEARS

The purpose of a broker is to facilitate the trade. After you open a trading account, the broker gives a trader the right to execute transactions, which includes certain rights and privileges, including the right to be a bull or a bear. The terms *bull* and *bear* were created by traders in the stock market in the early 1900s to identify the direction someone was trading in the market. The term *bull* was derived from the way in which bulls attack or charge, moving upward. In contrast, *bears* move downward when they attack or charge.

Bulls, therefore, resemble a buying market, because they believe prices will continue to move upward, or rise, whereas bears resemble a selling market, because they believe prices are going move downward, or fall. Every trader has to make a decision to be either a bull or a bear before entering the market. Bulls enter the market buying (first) and exit selling (second). Bears do the opposite: they enter selling (first) and exit buying (second). To make a profit in the market, you must always buy low and sell high. Both bulls and bears are trying to do that; bears just reverse the transactions (see Figure 2-2).

TYPES OF ORDERS

There are four types of orders used in the market:

- *Market order*: This is an order placed to enter or exit the market at the current market price. Remember, there is a bid price and an ask price with a 3- to 6-pip spread on the major currencies (the U.S. dollar [USD], the Japanese yen [JPY], the British pound [GBP], the Swiss franc [CHF], the European euro [EUR], the Canadian dollar [CAD] and the Australian dollar [AUD]). Traders buy on the ask price and sell on the bid price. If we are trading the EUR/USD currency pair and prices are bid 1.2810 at ask 1.2813, there is a 3-pip

FIGURE 2-2   EUR/USD (One Hour Chart) Bull and Bear Price Movement

spread. If you want to enter buying, you would pay the ask price of 1.2813 and if you wanted to enter selling, you would sell at 1.2810. The current bid/ask price is called the market price and entering at one of those prices is called a market order.

- *Limit orders*: Orders used to enter or exit the market at a predetermined price are called limit orders. You can enter and exit the market using a limit order, which are orders placed ahead of time to enter the market buying below where current prices are or selling above where the current prices are. A limit order is better known as "the order placed to get out of the market for a profit after you enter."

- *Stop orders*: Similar to limit orders, stop orders are also used to enter and exit the market but have a different set of rules attached to them. They are placed like a limit order at a predetermined price; however, they turn into market orders when the market reaches the predetermined price and may be subjected to *slippage*.

Slippage occurs when you place a stop order at a certain price and the market moves faster than the broker can execute the order and you receive a *worse* fill. The rule is, when you place a buy order above the current market price it is called a *stop order*, and when you place a sell order below where the current price is it is also called a *stop order*. Most stop orders are known as "the order placed to exit the market at a loss after you enter"—the order used to protect your principal equity.

- *OCO orders*: Before any trader enters the market, they must create a trading plan and follow it. Every trade should have an entry point, a predetermined exit point for profit, and a well-thought-out exit point for minimal loss should the market not go your way. The rule is, every buy order should have two sells: a sell limit order for profit and a sell stop order for loss protection. Conversely, every sell order should have two buy orders: a buy limit order for profit and a buy stop order for loss protection. Some trading software programs allow the trader the ability to place an OCO (one cancels the other) order. This means the moment the market hits either the stop order or the sell order, it cancels the opposite order. By trading with an OCO order, you are not left exposed with a working order after either your stop or limit has been filled and you have been taken out of the market. An OCO order offers you the opportunity to set a trade and forget about it. You can literally walk away from your computer and not be concerned with catastrophic results if you have properly quantified your potential losses before you placed the trade. No one knows where the next pip will go, so the best you can do is plan your trade and trade your plan.

One of the most important and productive habits you can adopt is properly educating yourself about the Forex before you begin trading. If you move forward without the proper education, be prepared to lose your money, much like in a casino. You will be trading off your "gut feel" and emotion and placing yourself in the same position as that of a reckless gambler. Just like the casino, the market will be there to take all your money.

I have learned that to achieve success in trading requires learning to understand the three critical facets of trading:

1. The technical education and trading knowledge
2. The fundamental understanding of what determines market movement
3. The psychological side of trading—the most important aspect

THE MARKET TRADERS INSTITUTE PHILOSOPHY

I founded Market Traders Institute (MTI) in 1994 and am now commonly known in the industry as "FXCHIEF," having trained more than 15,000 students since then.

All successful traders learn that working through frustration is the path to success. Knowing what to do when you get frustrated is critical. Learning to overcome and master your frustrations in life, as well as in trading, is an important part of a trader's armor.

Strong people make as many mistakes as weak people. The difference is that strong people admit their mistakes, laugh at them, and learn from them, and that is how they become strong. Mistakes are part of being human. We need to appreciate our mistakes for what they are. Just about all of life's important lessons can only be learned the hard way, by making mistakes.

Before you begin trading, you need to create your own mission statement to help you focus on becoming an educated, financially successful, long-term Forex trader. I want you to think of your journey toward becoming a successful trader as a transformation of thought, a new process of knowledge build-up, followed by:

1. Disciplined thought
2. Disciplined rules
3. Disciplined action

THE THREE LEVELS OF TRADING

LEVEL 1: THE BEGINNER TRADER
Your focus is on studying, understanding, and beginning to establish your trader's constitution, methodology, and trading strategy to match your personality. Practice first on a demo account to become comfortable with the trading platform before trading with real money.

LEVEL 2: THE COMPETENT TRADER
You acquire conscious competence. You begin to trade with real money, work through your emotions, and learn to trade within the equity management rules to achieve a consistent financial return.

LEVEL 3: THE EXPERT TRADER
You acquire unconscious competence. You mechanically execute profitable trades with no emotion. Your decisions are based on your belief,

education, established rules, and experiences to achieve a consistent financial return.

THE REALITY OF TRADING

The reality of trading is that less than 10 percent of all traders who attempt to trade succeed in the market. More than 90 percent of all traders who attempt to become successful on the Forex fail.

Our professional international team at Market Traders Institute adamantly believes in proper education first. Knowledge is the key that can make a big difference in the success of a trader, providing a necessary edge. In this market:

Knowledge = income
Lack of knowledge = lack of income
Correctly applied, knowledge can = financial freedom!

I cannot stress this enough: the majority of the world is locked into managing its poverty or mediocrity. Very few people learn how to manage any kind of success because they are not given any sort of manual or instruction guide to success. Growing up, we learn how to survive financially from our caregivers and circles of influence. But not all mentors are successful, leaving many to learn through trial and error.

Thousands of books have been written on how to achieve some sort of success. I believe that success comes from acquiring the right education about the opportunity; possessing the right work ethic; implementing the right productive daily habits; and believing with focus, concentration, action, and a positive attitude that your dream will come true. Successful people keep things simple. They find beauty in simplicity. The average person, for some reason, tries very hard to complicate things, even the simplest processes or procedures. I, on the other hand, have worked hard to take a very complicated issue, Forex, and simplify it, enabling just about anyone to understand how the markets work and how to trade them.

THE 21-DAY, 3 PERCENT RULE

The human mind forgets 80 percent of the knowledge it acquires within the first three days of acquisition. During the next 18 days, it continues the loss of information until it settles at 3 percent retention of the new information.

In other words, "if you don't use it, you will lose it." This discovery was made after years of research and has affected how our company does business. Our focus at MTI is to provide you with productive practical, continued education, enabling you to be trading with 90-percent-plus recall. We provide our clients with the MTI trader's checklist, enabling them to cover 100 percent of all the trading issues before they trade, just as a pilot covers his flight checklist before he takes off.

CONCLUSION

Understanding all successful trading procedures and rules before you trade is essential for your success. You must practice them over and over again until they become an unconscious habit. Doctors do not start operating on their patients after a semester in school, and pilots don't fly passengers around the world after a weekend class of learning how to fly. Doctors practice on cadavers first. They practice a long time before they are allowed to perform any operations—for the simple reason that other people's lives depend on their actions. Pilots fly with instructors long before they go solo. The same reasoning and rules apply to trading: although you might not lose your life if you don't know what you are doing when you trade, you most certainly can lose your financial stability.

3

SELF-EMPOWERMENT VIA TRADING SOFTWARE

THE VALUE OF SELF EMPOWERMENT

Learning to trade successfully on the Forex is about self-empowerment and independence. I personally believe that self-empowerment is learning how to fish and that dependency is all about being handed a fish to stay alive. I know there are many companies out there offering education, trading strategies, and even trading systems that claim to take you from "rags to riches" in a short period of time. Make no mistake, there is no holy grail! You cannot buy any indicator or trading system that works 100 percent of the time any more than the airlines can buy an autopilot system that eliminates the need for pilots. If you are being courted by any company that is leading you to believe you can buy a trading system with buy and sell signals that will take you from "rags to riches," you will be greatly disappointed.

Let us say you created a trading system that worked 95 percent of the time or that allowed you to double your money every few months just by following the trading signals. If you created such a trading system, would you sell it for $1,000? or $3,000, $5,000, $10,000, or even $50,000? I would think not, because if you could create such a trading system, all you would need to do is walk into any major financial institution like the Bank of America or the Royal Bank of Scotland and show proof that your automated system works. If it did, the bank would likely be willing to pay you $1 billion or more for it.

Just as there is no perfect trading system, there is no autopilot system that works without a pilot. I very much doubt that human beings will ever put their lives on the line with a computer or autopilot system in an airplane without a pilot. We all have bought enough electronic equipment in our lives—TVs, VCRs, cameras, and so forth—to know they all fail eventually. Don't put your hard-earned money in a get-rich-quick scheme.

Pilots are educated and trained to fly proficiently before they are even shown where the autopilot system button is. I will never forget back in 1984 when I got my private pilot's license. The first time I got into the cockpit with my instructor I asked him where the autopilot button was. He looked at me and said, "If you ever ask me that question again before you get your private pilot's license, I will throw you out of my class." Well, I never asked that question again, even after I got my license. I did eventually learn how to engage the autopilot function and will have to say, the autopilot system is not a fail-safe function without the close monitoring of a pilot. As powerful as such systems are, when things start to go wrong, they cannot make spilt-second decisions in the best interest of the passengers. They can only do what they are programmed to do, and there are too many variables in flying to program absolutely everything. Autopilot systems do not work 100 percent of the time, they have their limitations.

As a trader, you will learn that, from time to time, the trading environment will be ideal enough to use an autopilot system. There are some good ones, but they don't work all the time. You need to realize that the market can turn turbulent at any time, and if, all of a sudden, it does turn turbulent, you will have to have the capability to sit in the captain's chair and bring the aircraft back to the airport without any major incident. That is truly successful trading.

I will never forget September 11, 2001. I was sitting in my office at home and had been in a few trading positions for a couple of days on four different currencies. All of a sudden, they all took off like rockets in the opposite direction of my positions. Thank goodness I was not using an auto-pilot trading system or I could have been financially wiped out that day. I was stopped out on all four currencies and was able to preserve what profit I had made.

The reality is that to become a successful trader, you must go through an education process no different than that of becoming a pilot, a physician, or of any profession that requires a specific discipline to be mastered.

I never cease to be amazed at all the "marketing gurus" who start Forex education training companies or attempt to sell Forex "buy and sell signals" and prey on the ignorant by promising them untold fortunes on the Forex for the bargain price of $995. I am even more amazed at the massive amounts of people willing to purchase these products. But I am never surprised when they call our office and share their experience of buying a Forex program that failed or disappointed them. These traders are now pleading for help because with their current system, they keep on losing money and have no idea how to make it back. Clearly, what they purchased doesn't work for them in the market.

I guess experience is what you get when you don't get what you want. A fair question is, did the system truly fail or was it the system found between their ears that failed?

You must be taught how to use the best tools available for whatever profession you want to pursue. If you are going to be a ditch digger, you need to be taught how to use a backhoe as well as a shovel and be taught in which situations one or the other should be used.

Learning to trade on Forex, from someone who is already successful at trading, is critical. Finding out which trading tools they use is equally important. Now is not the time to go bargain hunting for tools. Bargain hunting for free or low-cost trading tools is like learning to navigate on the ocean with a compass in a 12-foot canoe—clearly the wrong vessel for the environment. A solid built, 1,100-foot, state-of-the-art cruise ship with all the latest gauges for weather would be wiser. With so much at stake, do not take a shortcut on paying for quality trading tools.

When it comes to trading on Forex, I highly recommend the MTI 4.0 charting package (see Figure 3-1).

FIGURE 3-1   Four Major Currency Pairs on Four-Hour Time Frame Charts (EUR/USD; GBP/USD; CHF/USD; JPY/USD)

It has more than 150 trading indicators that can be used in creating trading systems that align with your trading personality. These systems can be back-tested over many years instantaneously, allowing a trader to see if their trading strategy is a good one, or if they are working in the wrong direction. You can create a trading strategy that aligns with your personality, program it into a system, back-test it, and, if it is productive, have the trading system send you alerts via e-mail or cell phone when an entry and or exit signal is triggered (see Figure 3-2).

The most important part about a trading system is that it must be simple and easy to use. Whether it is done visually or created by a trading system, your trading strategy must have three very important components:

1. It must be able to find the current market direction.
2. It must have a consistent entry strategy that works consistently.
3. It must have two very clear exit strategies, one for protecting you against major losses and one for capturing a profit.

FIGURE 3-2   EUR/USD (One-Hour Chart)

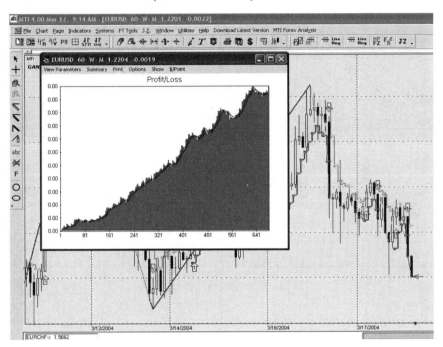

HOW TO DETERMINE MARKET DIRECTION

The MTI 4.0 charting program helps traders determine market direction. In Figure 3-3, you can see a line that goes above and below the price movement against time that is monitored by a computer creating a candlestick formation (candlestick formations are a way of monitoring the open, high, low, and close market prices in any given time period). This line is called a *moving trend line*; a visual indicator of market direction or perhaps the current trend. When you turn on your computer and begin to review your charts on any time frame, if the current candle is above that line, the market on that time frame is in a potential uptrend, and if the current candle is below that line, the market on that time frame is in a potential downtrend.

No matter what time frame you trade in, this simple exercise accompanied with this system can help you determine trend direction.

The indicators on a chart can become like the autopilot button on an airplane, however, as discussed previously, airplanes don't fly themselves—they need pilots. Before you use an autopilot program, you need to understand how it has been programmed.

FIGURE 3-3   EUR, CHF, GBP, JPY/USD (Four-Hour Charts)

FIGURE 3-4   Indicators and Oscillators

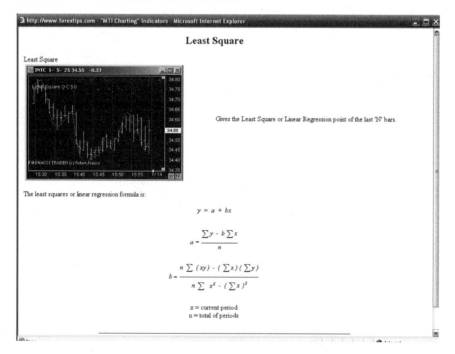

Least Square

Gives the Least Square or Linear Regression point of the last 'N' bars.

The least squares or linear regression formula is:

$$y = a + bx$$

$$a = \frac{\sum y - b \sum x}{n}$$

$$b = \frac{n \sum (xy) - (\sum x)(\sum y)}{n \sum x^2 - (\sum x)^2}$$

x = current period
n = total of periods

Indicators and oscillators (which are nothing more than mathematical equations that are monitoring price movement against time displayed via lines on a chart; see Figure 3-4) are one way to determine market direction. Looking at the moving trend line, on any time frame, can help you determine market direction on that time frame.

One mistake traders often make is believing that a trading system created for a 30-minute chart will work on all time frames, such as a one-hour chart or a daily chart. Sometimes it does work, but typically, as you move a trading system from one time frame to another, you may want to adjust the settings of such a system to optimize its performance on that time frame. It is vital to find trading software that will not only allow you to change these settings but also instantaneously back-test the results as found incorporated in MTI 4.0.

USING INDICATORS TO DETERMINE AN ENTRY POINT

Once you have determined market direction, you need an entry trading strategy that works more times than not. Every trader wants the market to move in his or her direction from entry—there is nothing worse than getting in a trade and having the market run in the opposite direction. One of the most important traits of a successful person is that when they are trying to make a productive, empowered decision, they gather facts. The more facts they can gather, the more informed their decision.

Trading is 10 percent skill and 90 percent emotion, which is why our emotions frequently stand in the way of making good decisions. Anytime you need to make a decision, do yourself a favor and *do not* make it while you are in an emotional state. Take the time to calm down and place yourself in a logical state of mind. If you do that, you will open up the left side of your brain, where all your knowledge is stored, where all your intellectual recall is, and you will have access to everything you have learned in your past that is productive. You will begin to make an educated, positive, and productive decision.

Trading indicators can keep you from using the right side of your brain, where all your emotions are stored. You can program buy and sell signals that have no emotion, they just monitor price movement against time.

Using different indicators together can create effective entry points, like the ones found in Figure 3-5, but they need to be manually monitored. The trading system you are looking at in Figure 3-5 is called the MTI Trend Scalper.

The two moving lines overlapping the candles are moving trend lines, which can act as buy and sell signals. The line closest to the candles is a moving inner trend line and the other one is a moving outer trend line.

FIGURE 3.5   EUR/USD (Daily Chart)

When the inner trend line crosses over from the north to the south, it is time to sell, and when it crosses over from the south to the north, it is time to buy.

In Figure 3-5 (top), you can see that if you used the moving trend lines as your entry and exit signals, right around March 10, 2006, you would have bought the euro at approximately 1.2000, or when the lines crossed, and sold it around June 15, 2006, at 1.2800, when the lines crossed again for an 800-pip gain. That is an $8,000 profit from a $1,000 investment from a three-month trade (which is considered long-term trading).

But where do you get in if the moving trend lines have already crossed? Do you have to sit there for another three to six months before they cross over again to find another trading opportunity? The answer is no. You can have two options. You either educate yourself how the markets move without using indicators or you learn to add additional indicators to your trading system like the waving line you see at the bottom of the chart in Figure 3-5. This indicator, called the MTI Trend Tracker, monitors the waves of the market. As the market moves, it resembles the waves of the ocean. The market does not just take off in one direction, it waves as it moves, rallying and retracing, ebbing and flowing, three steps up, two steps back, three steps up, perhaps one and one-half steps back before it goes back up again as it creates its trend making higher highs and higher lows.

The greatest part about a trading system is that it is constantly monitoring the movement of the market, projecting directions with entry and exit points 24 hours a day even while you sleep or work. Using a trading system allows you to control your trading in the market, rather than the market controlling you, and to come and go, or turn off your computer, without having to do all kinds of new technical analysis of the market to catch up from where you left off.

If the lines overlapping the candles crossed while you were away, the MTI Trend Tracker allows you to enter the market at a price point where the market will more than likely reverse and rally back up in your buying direction from entry, which is what every trader wants. Look at the MTI Trend Tracker indicator where you see the bold up-arrows (see Figure 3-5, bottom). When the moving line is going south and then U-turns to the north, the market should follow. Look at the price movement of the market and how it began to rally again. This trading system works just as effectively in a downtrend as it does in an uptrend, as you can see in Figure 3-6. All the rules are the same but in the opposite direction.

When the lines overlapping the candles cross from the north to the south, it is time to sell. Once again, if you turn on your charts and the moving trendlines have already crossed, giving a short signal, you can enter when the MTI Trend Tracker indicator moving north U-turns to the south. Look at the market movement on the charts after the U-turn toward the south. Using trading indicators eliminates a lot of the guessing and allows you to focus on developing a trading strategy that works consistently, on a time frame that suits your personality. Some traders like fast action and want to turn their computer into a video game—they want to quickly scalp the market. In and out, in and out, perhaps 10 times a day. If you're one of those traders who enjoys scalping the market, you may want to trade using 5-minute to 30-minute time frames or charts. If you enjoy day trading, use this trading system on one-hour to four-hour time frames, and if you enjoy long-term trading, use this trading system on four-hour, daily, or weekly charts In any of these cases, you let the computer do the majority of the work.

It looks easy, doesn't it? Just like an autopilot system. If it were that easy, however, we would all be living in gated communities and flying our jets to our beach-house estates every weekend. Of course, it isn't.

Most traders make their money during trends and lose it when the market gets turbulent or begins to go sideways. Sideways movement in the

FIGURE 3-6   EUR/USD (Daily Chart)

market is when the market begins to bracket or consolidate creating equal highs and equal lows for a period of time (see Figure 3-7). What if you were just starting out and the market began to go sideways, or consolidate, as shown in Figure 3-7. Just about every time the computer gave a buy signal, the market went south, and just about every time the computer gave a sell signal, the market reversed and went north. When most people board an airplane and look inside the cockpit, they are intimidated by all the gauges they see. They say to themselves, "I could never do that." But the reality is, they could. How do I know? I used to say the same thing when I boarded those same planes, and I am proud to report that I received my private pilot's license back in 1984. Just like when I turned on my computer back in the 1980s and looked at charts, I, too, was extremely intimidated. But believe it or not, sideways movement can potentially offer the trader more trading opportunities than trends. Envision buying all the lows as seen in Figure 3-7 and exiting at the highs and then reversing your position, shorting the market by selling all the highs taking a ride across the trading channel and exiting at the lows. It is clear to see by continually repeating this process that there is profit to be made.

FIGURE 3-7   EUR/USD (One-Hour Chart)

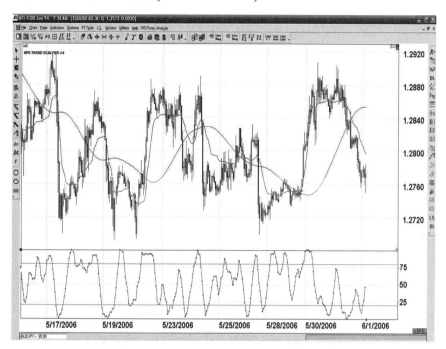

USING INDICATORS TO DETERMINE EXIT STRATEGIES

When going long in the market or buying first to enter the market, every buy entry order needs two sell exit orders, one for profit and one for loss. Conversely, when going short or selling first to enter the market, every sell entry order needs two buy exit orders, one for profit and one for loss. After you enter the market, you need the two exit points, one for profit and one for financial protection should the trade not work out. The fact of the matter is that no one knows where the next pip will go. The best you can do is to understand how the market works and learn how to go with it. It's like navigating in the ocean—it can be predictable at times and very unpredictable at others. But success comes to those who understand how it works—just look at the people who have been able to create great companies that haul freight, passengers, or oil over the ocean.

After the market has moved in your direction from entry, as planned, the question is where do you get out? The last thing in the world you want to do is guess what the market is going to do next. Let a simple mathematical calculation of price movement against time tell you instead.

You can use your indicators to make your exit decisions as well. Remember the two indicators—the moving trend lines that are overlapping the candles and the MTI Trend Tracker at the bottom of the chart? If you take a long position and want to become a long-term trader, you may want to stay in until the moving trend lines cross over. However, if you only want to grab a few pips, and you entered using the indicator below, you may want to get out after that line has moved from the south to the north and is beginning to U-turn back south (see Figure 3-8).

Some traders use the movement of their indicators as their protective stop loss orders—they let the indicators make their decisions regarding when to reverse their positions. I don't recommend this, because you are letting your emotions make your decisions. How? If you do not have a clearly defined exit point, you will get caught up in the "hope and fear trap." Once the market moves against you, and you are relying on the indicator to tell you what to do to get out with a small loss, well, guess what? Your hope and or fear will get the best of you. The best place to put your protective

FIGURE 3-8   EUR/USD (Daily Chart)

stops are a little beyond the latest major level of support or the last low if going long and a little beyond the latest major level of resistance or the last high if going short. What is critical is finding and calculating where your protective stop order needs to go as you are making your trading plan. Once you find that location, after you enter the market, place that order immediately and *do not move it* if you are trading an OCO (one cancels the other) order.

Trading is about keeping your losses small and letting your profits run.

The problem with most Forex traders is they hold onto their losses and quickly dump their profits for fear the market will take them back. They have the definitions of hope and fear backwards. They will hold a losing position for days, sweating it out, walking through the valley in the shadow of death, praying, hoping, promising God and everyone else that will listen to just help them get back to breakeven and once they do, they dump their position after only capturing a few pips. Some traders will go 300 pips in the red to only exit after a brutal ordeal and capture only 2 pips.

Learning where to place your protective stop loss orders and creating a trading plan before you trade is of critical importance as a novice trader. Below are some trading tips for novice traders;

- Keep your exit strategy simple and never risk more than you are willing to make.

- Trade using smaller time frames—perhaps 30-minute, 15-minute, or 10-minute time frames. Trade a simple strategy with a clear entry order accompanied by two exit orders trying to capture a profit of perhaps 10 to 20 pips. That is $10 to $20 in profit on a mini ($10,000) account and $100 to $200 on a regular ($100,000) account.

- As a beginner trader, you want to set a goal of trading 7 out of 10 times successfully, making more money than you lose by trading on smaller time frames, before moving to larger time frames. Your aim should be to establish the habit of winning more than you are losing. After you get in the habit of winning more than losing, and realizing that losing is just as much a part of this game as winning, you will then be able to move to a larger time frame to capture more pips, perhaps capturing 40 to 80 pips at a time, consistently, 7 out of 10 times with some losses.

- The most important part of this process is forming successful trading habits. After you get the simple basics down of winning more than losing, you can start learning more advanced exit strategies.

USING MULTIPLE TIME FRAMES TO TRADE

As you look at multiple time frames, always remember that the movements on the smaller time frames are controlled by the movements on the larger time frames. Take two different time frames, for example, a daily time frame and a four-hour time frame, using the same MTI Trend Scalper trading system on both time frames.

Remember the MTI Trend Tracker at the bottoms of the charts, which monitors the wave movement? Look what happens to the price movement on a four-hour chart when the indicator U-turns on a daily chart, as seen in Figure 3-9. The prices U-turned on the four-hour chart, didn't they? Remember, prices on a smaller time frame respond to the movement on a larger time frame. This works the same on all time frames and is a great way to trade.

CONCLUSION

All successful traders create a trading plan and trade their plan. After you create a trading plan, cross-check it with the MTI "Grade Your Trade

FIGURE 3-9   EUR/USD Charts

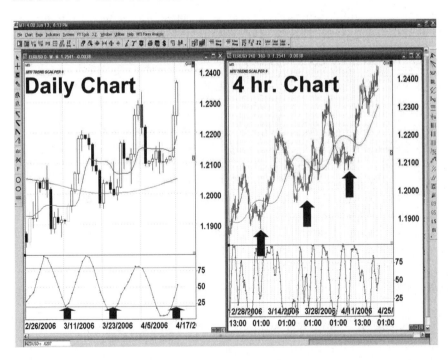

FIGURE 3-10   EUR/USD (One-Hour Chart)

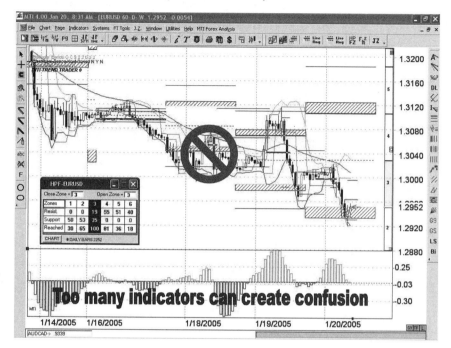

Checklist," The MTI "Grade Your Trade Checklist" allows you to attach percentages to the probability of success of your trade. The MTI checklist cross-checks important points for your entry and exit. These seven points are graded, indicating the odds of your making money, and include the use of indicators, candlestick formations, Fibonacci (Fib) numbers, countertrend lines, and more.

Trading needs to be fun and simple. Anyone who tries to impress you with all their knowledge and indicators (see Figure 3-10) will only confuse you.

A confused mind is going to take you down a path of financial destruction. Stay clear from using too many indicators or complicated indicators. *Keep it simple!*

C H A P T E R 4

TRADING
JAPANESE
CANDLESTICKS

CHARTS MAY BE deaf and mute, yet they still communicate very well. Candlestick formations are the sign language of the market. They frequently tell the trader where U-turns or reversals are and where the market is going.

Most beginner traders prefer learning how to read charts using what is called a Japanese candlestick, which monitors price movement against time. There are three types of charts traders can refer to: a line chart, a bar chart, or a candlestick chart. Until recently, bar charts dominated the financial industry, but now even the world's top traders are using Japanese candlestick charts for the additional information they can provide.

THE HISTORY OF JAPANESE CANDLESTICKS

The period 1500 to 1600 in Japan was known as Sengoku Jidai, or The Age of War. Military confrontation had become a way of life in that country as feudal lords fought for control of rival territories.

Over a period of 40 years (1534–1582, 16th century), three charismatic generals—Nobunaga Oda, Hideyoshi Toyotumi, and Leyasu Tokagawa—unified Japan. Once somewhat relative peace had been established, several new opportunities for expansion developed.

It was during 1600 that the concept of the Japanese candlestick was being explored, tested, and used in monitoring prices in the rice markets. Because there was no standardized currency, the price of rice became the predominant medium of exchange, or currency. In the late 1600s, the Rice Exchange was formed to regulate trading proceedings. By 1710, there were more than 1,300 rice dealers. Rather than just deal in actual rice, rice coupons were issued, and these became one of the first forms of futures contracts ever traded.

Similar events took place in other parts of the world. There was the Tulip Mania that swept The Netherlands in the early 1600s, which also involved a form of futures contract. During this period, tulips became the standard medium of exchange and became even more valuable than gold there.

The popularity of these Tulip coupons were drawing attention around the world and other countries began to catch on to this effective way of trading. Rice coupons in Japan became significant, with a bale of rice being the standard amount to be traded. By 1749, there were approximately 110,000 bales of rice traded via "empty rice coupons" although it is believed there were only about 30,000 bales in all of Japan. An empty rice coupon became a form of a futures contract—a coupon for rice that may not even be planted or harvested yet. The rice is traded for a specific future date, as if it was grown and going to be delivered to that person on that future date. Today, futures trading is a multibillion dollar industry. In America, most futures trading for commodities occurs in Chicago, at the Chicago Mercantile Exchange, or CME.

But where do Japanese candlesticks fit in? Munehisa Homma was born into a wealthy Japanese farming family in 1724. Homma had an aptitude for business and would eventually become a dominant trader in the Japanese rice market. Although candlesticks were not actually developed by Homma, he studied the psychology of investors and formulated several key trading principles. These concepts evolved into the candlestick charting techniques that we know today.

Candlestick charts were originally plotted painstakingly by hand. This labor-intensive step, as well as the fact that many Japanese traders could not properly communicate or share their trading methods due to language barriers, meant that the use of Japanese candlestick formations could not become widespread until recent times. However, they are now included in the majority of financial charting packages as a standard option and are a key indicator for establishing a method of prices and analyses, alongside the more traditional bar charts and line charts.

HOW TO READ A JAPANESE CANDLESTICK

Japanese candlestick charts monitor price movement during a certain period of time. As the candlesticks form, they begin to tell a story of the activity in the market, as well as reflect the mood of the market during that time. Candlesticks become the sign language of the market, communicating via certain formations the future potential moves of the market, which is how profits are made—by projecting correctly where the market will go, not where it has been.

Successful traders take the time to study and understand this visual language. Candlestick formations indicate clear buy and sell signals, communicating to the trader when it is time to enter the market or to get out. How well you understand candlestick formations can give you a significant advantage in the market.

Japanese candlesticks formations can provide the trader with the market's first sign of changing direction, a coming U-turn, or a reversal. They will appear in the form of a single candlestick or a combination of more than one candlestick. There are hundreds of formations, yet only a handful of formations carry substantial weight when looking for a good entry point. A good entry point is described as a location where the market goes your way from the beginning. Let us see what a Japanese candlestick looks like and how it forms (see Figure 4-1).

Candlesticks, which are composed of full bodies and wicks, measure price fluctuations within a certain period of time. As prices move up or down from the opening, the body begins to form. If, from the opening price, prices move up and then close higher than the opening, it is a bullish candle. These candlesticks, in this book, will always appear "empty" or "white"—which indicates their bullish nature. If prices begin to fall from the opening price and close lower than the opening, it is a bearish candle. These candlesticks will always appear to be "filled" or "black" in this book—which indicates their Bearish nature. The lines on the north and south sides of the bodies of the candles are called "wicks." They monitor the highest price, or high, and the lowest price, or low, of that time period. For example, you can set your charts to provide you with 5-minute candlesticks, 10-, 15-, or 30-minute candlesticks, even hourly, daily, weekly, monthly, or yearly. Candlesticks monitor price movement against time, providing traders with four key pieces of information for that specific time period: the opening price, the closing price, the highest price reached, and the lowest price reached.

FIGURE 4-1

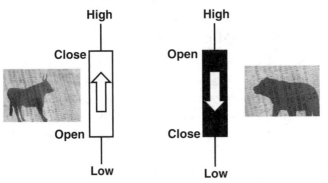

Reading Japanese Candlesticks

Candlesticks measure price fluctuations
within a certain time frame.

Copyright 2005 by Market Traders Institute, Inc.

Trading is a financial game involving two opponents: the bulls and bears. We all know that there are not actual bulls and bears trading in the market, but investors and traders who have invested either in a bullish direction or a bearish direction. Both sides have clear objectives and want the market to move in their direction: bulls want the market to go up, or rally, to make higher highs, whereas the bears want to take the market down, or have it dip to make lower lows.

READING A JAPANESE CANDLESTICK CHART

Most novice traders look at Japanese candlestick charts simply because they are easy to read and understand. The numbers to the far right indicate the price and the numbers at the bottom of the chart indicate the time period. The very last candle to the right is the current candle, indicating the current price. All the previous candles, to the left of the current candle, have recorded the historic price movement during that time. As you see in Figure 4-2, all the icons to the left, top, and right of the actual chart are your trading tools.

HOW TO FIND A HIGH

Highs are defined as a level where the market ceases to rally and U-turns in the opposite direction. You can spot a high between four candles, when the

FIGURE 4-2   USD/CHF (Four-Hour Chart)

two to the left and the two to the right are lower than the center wick, which is highest. A high can be considered a new level of resistance, or a higher price level achieved by the bulls that is interrupted and reversed by the bears.

However, not all highs are major levels of resistance. Only highs that are higher than the current market can be considered a level of resistance (see Figure 4-2).

The levels of resistance noted in the above chart as R1, R2, R3, R4, and R5 become future price targets for the bulls to chase and move higher. Once they regain control of the market, they will aim to make higher highs and higher lows. The bears are maintaining control in the above chart, as the market is making lower lows and lower highs.

HOW TO FIND A LOW

A low is defined as the level where the market ceases to drop. A low in a candlestick formation is seen where there are two candles to the left and two candles to the right that are higher than the center wick, which is the lowest

FIGURE 4-3   USD/CHF (One-Hour Chart)

point. A low can be considered as a new level of support, or a lower price level that was achieved by the bears and then interrupted and reversed by the bulls; however, only lows that are lower than the current market level can be considered a level of support (see Figure 4-3).

The levels of support noted in the above chart as S1, S2, S3, S4, and S5 become future targets for the bears to chase and/or move lower. Once they gain control of the market again, they will aim to make lower lows and lower highs. The bulls control the above market example.

UNDERSTANDING THE DIFFERENT JAPANESE CANDLESTICKS

The art of proper communication starts with taking the time to learn and educate yourself about the various forms of communication, including the spoken word, body language, and voice fluctuations, among others.

Although candlesticks may look alike, the 20 formations listed in Figure 4-4 will provide you with a solid understanding of candlestick formations and their meanings.

FIGURE 4-4   Japanese Candlesticks

BULLISH PATTERN		HAMMER. This is a bullish line if it occurs after a significant downtrend. If the line occurs after a significant uptrend, it is called a hanging man. A hammer is identified by a small body (a small range between the open and closing prices) and a long lower shadow (the low is significantly lower than the open, high, and closes). The body can be empty or filled in.
BULLISH PATTERN	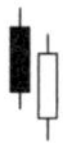	PIERCING LINE. This is a bullish pattern and the opposite of a dark cloud cover. The first line, on the left, is a bearish line, and the second line is a bullish line. The second line opens lower than the first line's low but closes more than halfway above the first line's real body.
BULLISH PATTERN		BULLISH ENGULFING LINES. This pattern is strongly bullish if it occurs after a significant downtrend (it acts as a reversal pattern). It occurs when a small bearish line is engulfed by a large bullish line.
BULLISH PATTERN	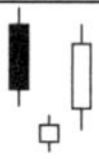	MORNING STAR. This is a bullish pattern signifying a potential bottom. The star, at the bottom between the two lines, indicates a possible reversal; the bullish line confirms this. The star can be empty or filled in.
BULLISH PATTERN		BULLISH DOJI STAR. A star indicates a reversal and a Doji indicates indecision. Thus, this pattern usually indicates a reversal after an indecisive period. You should wait for a confirmation, as in the morning star in the previous pattern, before trading a Doji star. The first line can be empty or filled in.
BEARISH PATTERN		HANGING MAN. These lines are bearish if they occur after a significant uptrend, and if the pattern occurs after a significant downtrend, it is called a hammer. They are identified by small real bodies (a small range between open and closing prices) and a long lower shadow, that is, the low was significantly lower than the open, high, and close. The bodies can be empty or filled in.

FIGURE 4-4   *Continued*

BEARISH PATTERN	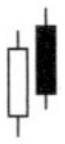	<u>DARK CLOUD COVER</u>. This is a bearish pattern that is more significant if the second line's body is below the center of the previous line's body (as illustrated).
BEARISH PATTERN		<u>BEARISH ENGULFING LINES</u>. This line is strong and bearish if it occurs after a significant uptrend—it acts as a reversal pattern. It occurs when a small bullish line is engulfed by a large bearish line.
BEARISH PATTERN	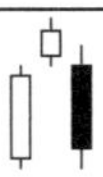	<u>EVENING STAR</u>. This is a bearish pattern signifying a potential top. The star indicates a possible reversal, and the bearish line confirms it. The star can be empty or filled in or it can be a Doji star.
BEARISH PATTERN		<u>DOJI STAR</u>. A star indicates a reversal and a Doji indicates indecision. Thus, this pattern usually indicates a reversal after an indecisive period. You should wait for a confirmation, such as an evening star illustration, before trading a Doji star.

BEARISH PATTERN		<u>SHOOTING STAR</u>. This pattern suggests a minor reversal when it appears after a rally. The star's body must appear near the low price, and the line should have a long upper shadow.
BEARISH PATTERN		<u>LONG-LEGGED DOJI</u>. This line often signifies a turning point. It occurs when the open and close are the same, and the range between the high and the low is relatively large.
BEARISH PATTERN		<u>DRAGONFLY DOJI</u>. This line also signifies a turning point. This pattern occurs when the open and the close are the same and the low is significantly lower than the open, high, and closing prices.

FIGURE 4-4   *Continued*

BEARISH PATTERN		GRAVESTONE DOJI. This line signifies another turning point. It occurs when the open, close, and low are the same, and the high is significantly higher than the open, low, and closing prices.
BEARISH PATTERN	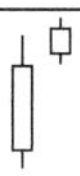	STAR. Stars indicate reversals. A star is a line with a small real body that occurs after a line with a much larger real body, where the real bodies do not overlap, although the shadows may.
NEUTRAL PATTERN		SPINNING TOPS. These are neutral lines. They occur when the distance between the high and the low, and the distance between the open and the close, are relatively small.
NEUTRAL PATTERN		DOJI. This line implies indecision because the security opened and closed at the same price. These lines can appear in several different patterns.
NEUTRAL PATTERN		DOUBLE DOJI. This implies a forceful move will follow a breakout from the current indecision.
NEUTRAL PATTERN		HARAMI ("pregnant" in English). This pattern indicates a decrease in momentum. It occurs when a line with a small body falls within the area of a larger body. In this example, a bullish line with a long body is followed by a weak bearish line and implies a decrease in the bullish momentum.

CANDLESTICK FORMATIONS

The market can only move in three directions: up, down, or sideways. When it moves, the candlesticks provide a visual sign that monitors the strength or weakness of the market in a certain direction. However, there are two basic types of candlesticks:

1.   Decision candlesticks
2.   Indecision candlesticks

Decision candlesticks are full-bodied bullish or bearish candles with relatively small wicks on either side. They communicate to the trader that either the bulls or the bears are in control. The indecision candlestick formation is exactly the opposite, with small bodies and, in some cases, no bodies at all—just a line where the open and the close were at the same price with large wicks on either side or on both sides (see Figure 4-5).

As the market moves, it creates visual waves, and the candlesticks form different patterns. Movements are caused by investors entering and exiting the market. When there are more buyers than sellers, the market begins to rally; when there are more sellers than buyers, the market begins to dip, or decline; and when there are equal numbers of buyers and sellers, the market goes sideways. These patterns communicate the strength or weakness of the continued move. The terms *rally* and *some dipping retracement* are used for a market increase, and the terms *dip* and *some rally retracement* are used in

FIGURE 4-5

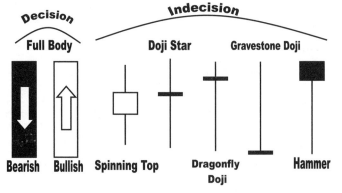

Candlestick Formations

a dip or fall in market prices. As the market moves, it waves, and the candlesticks form bullish and bearish reversal patterns. These patterns are the sign language of the market and the buy and sell signals for the traders. The patterns communicate when it is time to get in and when it is time to get out.

BULLISH CANDLESTICK FORMATIONS OR BUY SIGNALS

Even though there are many candlestick formations and patterns, there are three major bullish and three major bearish patterns that offer great buy and sell signals.

The three major bullish candlestick patterns are

- A morning star

- A bullish engulfing pattern

- A tweezer bottom

These formations will appear in an uptrend as well as in a downtrend, but they are of great value and offer great financial return if spotted and traded in an uptrend. These patterns can become invaluable whenever they appear at the end of a downtrend in a smaller time frame, which many times is nothing more than the end of a retracement in a larger time frame. It is imperative to note that as the market moves sideways in a 20- to 40-pip trading range, the market may form all kinds of bullish and bearish candlestick patterns, which should be ignored. It is imperative *not to trade* these candlestick formations in small consolidated or sideways movement.

The charts being used in this book have black and white candles—the black candles are bearish and the white are bullish.

THE MORNING STAR (BUY SIGNAL)

Figure 4-6 A clearly shows the formation of the morning star. What is important to note is that in the formation of morning stars, they start out with a bearish decision candle, followed by one, two, three, or even four indecision candles before the decision bullish candle appears. In Figure 4-6B, a morning star appears at the bottom of the chart, signifying the end of the recent dip. A morning star forms when you have a large bearish decision candle followed by one or more indecision candles, which are followed by a bullish decision candle that closes beyond the 60 percent mark, or beyond the top half of the beginning bearish decision candle. It indicates the market is U-turning. If the last bullish candle closes below the

FIGURE 4-6

(A)

Morning Star Formations

- This is a bullish pattern signifying a potential bottom and a potential reversal. Morning stars come in many shapes and can consist of more than 3 candles

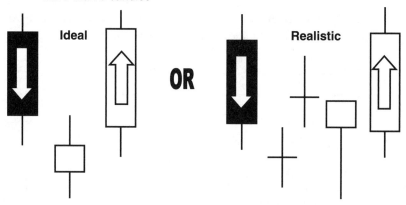

Ideal   OR   Realistic

(B)

USD/CHF (One-Hour Chart)

halfway point of the first bearish candle of the formation, it is a sign of continued bearish sentiment.

Investor Psychology Behind the Morning Star

The bears are losing control and investors are no longer selling when you spot a morning star. More buyers have come into the market, which creates an equal number of buyers and sellers. In the end, more buyers step in and take control of the market. Bears are placed in hibernation, and bulls come out of their corrals in herds. The final bullish candle of the formation sends ripples of greed throughout the trading community and a major rally takes place, especially when accompanied by significant trading volume.

THE BULLISH ENGULFING PATTERN (BUY SIGNAL)

A bullish engulfing candlestick formation often signifies the end of a down move, or a reversal. It can also be the turning point or the end of the retracement in an uptrend (see Figure 4-7A). An ideal bullish engulfing candle is formed when the candle opens lower than the close of the previous bearish decision candle, engulfing the previous two or three bearish candles. This is a strong sign of a U-turn. The bulls are clearly taking control, as seen in Figure 4-7B.

FIGURE 4-7

(A)   *Bullish Engulfing Candle*

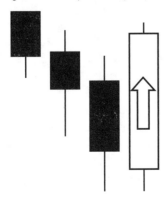

* Is a bullish candlestick formation that engulfs the previous bearish candle or candles after a downswing price move. The opening price of the bullish engulfing candle must be lower than the close of the previous bearish candle. The closing price of the bullish engulfing candle must be higher than the open of the previous bearish candle.

FIGURE 4-7   *Continued*

(B)

USD/CHF (Four-Hour Chart)

Investor Psychology Behind the Bullish Engulfing Pattern

The wind has been taken out of the bears' sails, and the bulls have arisen with increased stamina. Traders with short positions make a quick dash to cover their exposure, and their rush to exit their positions adds power to the creation of the pattern. The volume on the uptake component shows that the majority of traders have changed camp from bearish to bullish within the duration of one period.

TWEEZER BOTTOM BULLISH FORMATION (BUY SIGNAL)

Tweezer bottoms form when bears lose control. Buyers step in and create an environment of equal buyers and equal sellers, which forms two or more indecision candles. Figure 4-8A shows the formations.

When the market has been falling and a clear decision has been made by the bulls to take over, tweezer bottoms are formed. The market continues to move down, and bearish candles are formed. All of a sudden, an indecision candle appears, which means more bulls have started buying. We now have equal buyers and sellers. A tweezer bottom formation starts with a bearish decision candle, followed by perhaps one, two, three, even

FIGURE 4-8

(A)

Tweezer Bottom Formation

● This is a bullish pattern signifying a potential bottom and potential reversal. Tweezer bottoms can consist of 2 candles or more than 2 candles; bodies can be bullish / bearish or both; at least 2 candles must have long equal wicks that are found on the south side of the body of the candle. The wick on the south side of the body must be a minimum of 60% of the total candle.

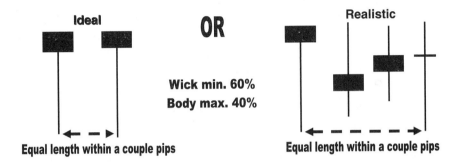

Ideal

OR

Realistic

Wick min. 60%
Body max. 40%

Equal length within a couple pips

Equal length within a couple pips

(B)

USD/CHF (One-Hour Chart)

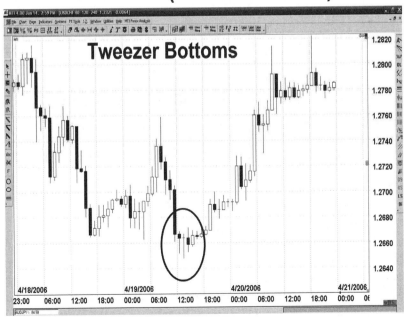

four indecision candles, as seen in Figure 4-8A. When bears attempt to take prices lower and bulls step in and buy more than bears, a long wick on the south side of a small-bodied candle forms. A second attempt is made by the bears to take prices lower, with the same results, leaving another indecision candle with a long wick on the south side of the small body of the indecision candle, next to the last one. The lows of the two candles, as displayed by the wicks, are usually at the same price or within a couple of pips difference, which now creates a new level of support. The tweezer bottoms scream out, "This is the end of this down move and the market is now getting ready to rally. Anyone wanting to make a profit in this next rally needs to start buying right now!" Why? Because higher prices are likely to follow the formation of tweezer bottoms, as you see in Figure 4-8B.

Invester Psychology Behind the Tweezer Bottoms

The bears have created lower prices, which have been tested, and new buyers have entered the market. As traders note more bullish participation, a rally is implied. The bears were unable to acquire the interest of more sellers and were not strong enough to hold prices down. Several attempts for lower prices failed, as evidenced by the long wicks on the south side of the small-bodied candles. The tweezer bottoms are a sign of selling exhaustion. It is important to note that the tweezer bottoms do not need to be side-by-side; they can be several candles apart, as long as the lows of the wicks are close to each other, with only a difference of a few pips. Such a formation will create a level of support.

BEARISH CANDLESTICK FORMATION OR SELL SIGNALS

The three major bearish candlestick patterns are

- An evening star

- A bearish engulfing pattern

- A tweezer top

These formations will appear in a downtrend as well as in an uptrend, but they are of great value and offer great financial return if spotted and traded in a downtrend. These patterns can become invaluable whenever they appear at the end of an uptrend in a smaller time frame, which many times is nothing more than the end of a retracement in a larger time frame. Once again, it is imperative to note that as the market moves sideways in a 20- to 40-pip trading range, the market may form all kinds of bullish and bearish candlestick patterns, which should be ignored. It is imperative that you remember *not to trade* these candlesticks formations in small consolidated or sideways movement.

THE EVENING STAR (SELL SIGNAL)

Figure 4-9A shows what an evening star looks like. What is important to note is that it starts out with a bullish decision candle, followed by perhaps one, two, three, even four indecision candles before the decision bearish candle appears.

In Figure 4-9B, an evening star appears at the top of the chart, signifying the end of the recent rally. An evening star forms when you have a large bullish decision candle, followed by one or more indecision candles, which are followed by a bearish decision candle that closes beyond the 60 percent mark, or beyond the bottom half of the beginning bullish decision candle. It signifies the market is U-turning. If the last bearish candle closes above the halfway point of the first bullish candle of the formation, it is a sign of continued bullish sentiment.

Investor Psychology Behind the Evening Star

In Figure 4-9B, the bulls start out rallying like a rocket going to the moon, driving prices higher. Initially, it seems nothing can stop them. These initial candles reinforce the bullish sentiment. All of a sudden, a spinning top appears—a sign of indecision—in the form of a small indecision candle. It is quickly followed by a bearish decision candle and the session quickly U-turns. The bulls lose control and investors are no longer buying. More sellers come into the market, which creates the dip in prices. Bulls run for cover and begin liquidating their bullish positions, which adds to the bearish momentum. In the end, more sellers step in and take control of the market. Bulls are corralled and bears come out of hibernation. The final bearish candle of the formation sends ripples of fear throughout the trading community and a major sell-off takes place, especially when accompanied by significant trading volume.

THE BEARISH ENGULFING PATTERN (SELL SIGNAL)

A bearish engulfing candlestick often signifies the end of an up move, or a reversal. It can also be the turning point or end of the retracement in a downtrend, as seen in Figure 4-10B. As prices continue to rally and the charts form small decision bullish candles, all of a sudden, a very large

FIGURE 4-9

(A)

Evening Star Formations

This is a bearish pattern signifying a potential top and potential reversal. Evening stars come in many shapes and can consist of more than 3 candles

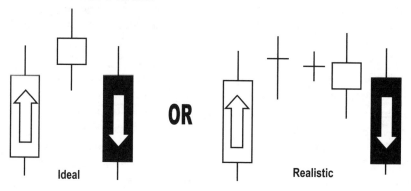

OR

Ideal   Realistic

(B)

USD/CHF (Four-Hour Chart)

FIGURE 4-10

(A)   # Bearish Engulfing Candle

- Is a bearish candlestick formation that engulfs the previous bullish candle or candles after an upswing price move. The opening price of the bearish engulfing candle must be higher than the close of the previous bullish candle and the closing price of the bearish engulfing candle must be lower than the open of the previous bullish candle.

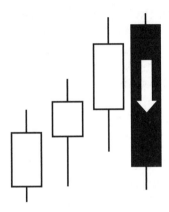

(B)   # USD/CHF (One-Hour Chart)

Bearish Engulfing Candles

decision bearish candle appears and literally engulfs the previous one to three bullish candles (see Figure 4-10A). The prototypical bearish engulfing candle occurs when the open of the bearish engulfing candle opens higher than the close of the previous bullish decision candles and engulfs several previous bullish candles. This is a strong sign of a U-turn when the bears are taking control.

Investor Psychology Behind the Bearish Engulfing Pattern

On an emotional level, a devastating blow has been swiftly delivered to the bulls when an engulfing bearish candle appears. Those feeling optimistic and buoyant about the upward market direction have been proverbially kicked in the teeth. Traders with long positions make a quick dash to cover their exposure, and their rush to exit their positions adds power to the creation of the bearish engulfing pattern. Within the duration of one period, the majority of traders have changed camp from a bullish perspective to a bearish orientation.

TWEEZER TOP FORMATION (SELL SIGNAL)

Tweezer tops form when bulls lose control. Sellers step in and balance out the numbers of buyers, which forms two or more indecision candles (see Figure 4-11A).

In Figure 4-11B, the market has been rallying, but a clear decision has been made by the bears to take over, observed via the formation of tweezer tops. As the market was moving up, bullish candles were forming. Then all of a sudden, an indecision candle appears, which means more bears have stepped in selling. There are now equal buyers and sellers. A tweezer top formation starts out with a bullish decision candle, followed by perhaps one, two, three, or even four indecision candles, as seen in Figure 4-11A. A tweezer top appears when the bulls attempt to take prices higher and bears step in and sell more than the bulls, creating a long wick on the north side of a small-bodied candle. A second attempt is made by the bulls to take prices higher, with the same results, leaving another indecision candle with a long wick, on the north side of the small body of the indecision candle next to the last one. The highs of the two candles, as displayed by the wicks, are usually at the same price or within a couple of pips difference, which now creates a new level of resistance. The tweezer tops scream out, "This is the end of this uptrend move and the market is now getting ready to dip. Anyone wanting to make a profit in this next dip needs to start selling right now!" Why? Because lower prices are likely to follow the formation of this pattern, as shown in Figure 4-11B.

FIGURE 4-11

(A)
Tweezer Top Formation

This is a bearish pattern signifying a potential top and potential reversal. Tweezer tops can consist of 2 candles or more than 2 candles; bodies can be bullish / bearish or both; at least 2 candles must have long equal wicks that are found on the north side of thebody of the candle. The wick on the north side of the body must be a minimum of 60% of the total candle.

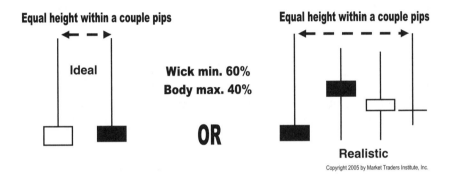

Equal height within a couple pips

Ideal

Wick min. 60%
Body max. 40%

OR

Equal height within a couple pips

Realistic

(B)
USD/CHF (Four-Hour Chart)

Investor Psychology Behind the Tweezer Tops

Bulls have made prices higher via their rally, however, bears, or more sellers, have entered the market. Indecision candles have formed next to each other and, in this case, three in a row, as seen in Figure 4-11B. With such resistance, the market collapses. With increased bearish participation, bears enter the market charging, and the result will be a dip. Shortly after the dip, the bulls try one last time to see if they can attract any more buying interest. The failed test by the bulls sends out the alarms, "Buyers are not strong enough to hold prices up—everyone sell!" The bulls are exhausted, and the bears take control. It is important to note that the failed attempt of the bulls to create higher prices formed the tweezer tops, although they do not need to be side by side.

TRADING CANDLESTICK PATTERNS

Learning how to identify and trade candlestick formations can be extremely useful in identifying potential coming patterns. However, although these patterns offer great trading signals, as seen in Figure 4-12,

FIGURE 4-12   Examples of Candlesticks Formations Daily EUR/USD Chart

you should not trade these candlesticks patterns on their merit alone. Your common sense is an excellent guide as well.

For example, your common sense should tell you that in a downtrend, only trade bearish candlestick formations, not bullish. Why? Because you are trading in the direction of the trend where the market strength is. You have a greater probability of the market moving in your direction after entry versus fighting against the trend. Obviously, you would do the opposite in an uptrend. When you trade in the direction of the trend, you will always have the market movement on your side, pushing the market in the direction of the current trend.

In trading any candlestick formation, you must wait until the last candle closes before you enter the market because the market may not necessarily react immediately after the candlestick formation has formed. Keep in mind that as long as you have your stop-loss orders in place, you are protected. The market will move on its own timetable—not yours. You have no control of the future movement of the market. No one knows where the next pip will go.

As long as the candles are above the outer moving uptrend line, you should enter buying bullish candlestick formations and exit selling bearish candlestick formations; the opposite applies in a downtrend. When the candles are below the outer moving trend line, enter selling bearish candlestick formations and exit buying bullish candlestick formations, as shown in Figure 4-12.

Trading is a game of probabilities and to put the probability of success in your favor, it is always helpful to compile more than one piece of evidence that the market will potentially U-turn and move in your direction at the price level you enter. In other words, success is increased if you have more than one educated reason to enter the market. When you have more than one good reason to enter a trade, that is what is called creating a convergence. This is, in essence, nothing more than building a case as to why the market is going to turn at that location.

Why is it that all of a sudden, at one number, the market creates a candlestick formation and changes direction or U-turns? It is almost as if there was a conspiracy taking place among a group of traders. We all know that is impossible, because there is no Forex building or pit filled with Forex traders who could manipulate prices. My sense is that nature must stay in balance, and nature takes whatever course it must to remain in balance. As human beings, we are part of nature and because we are the ones trading in the market, it is our buying and selling that make the movement in this market. The market is part of nature and will take whatever course it must to remain in balance, as you will see in Chapter 9.

CONCLUSION

I don't consider myself a religious man, but I am a spiritual man. I believe there is a greater power, perhaps a force of nature, orchestrating everything and everyone's outcome in this world. Nature can provide signs on our path to success of which I know most people never think about it. However, those individuals who try to understand it and tap into the potential it holds are the people who will benefit most and live fulfilling and wonderful lives. Conversely, those who just exist, living on automatic, never thinking about it, slowly become the victims of nature's balance because their focus is on survival.

I thought about all the trading opportunities I had missed over the years, due to the fact that I was not educated or ready to read the signs of success the market provided, like the evening stars and morning stars. If learning to become a successful trader is something you really want to achieve, you will need to prepare yourself to read the signs of the market. It is there you will find success.

5

THE FINANCIAL GAME OF SUPPORT AND RESISTANCE

I **NEVER THOUGHT IN MY** wildest dreams that trading in the financial markets was going to be a game, but it is. It is a game played on a daily basis by two teams, or two types of investors on opposite sides of a trade. The bulls want the market to go up. The bears want the market to go down. The two sides are in constant, unrelenting battle, fighting for control of the trading territory. Some make millions while others keep hoping the market will turn in their favor as they continue to root for their team—the bulls or the bears.

It sounds crazy when you hear that a trillion-dollar financial market works this way, but it does. Like any game in our lives, there are objectives, rules, and penalties. Each side is trying to get ahead by scoring points, following the rules of the game. You must obey the rules if you are planning to succeed in trading. If you break them, you are more than penalized—you fail.

On one of my trips to Australia, I bought a book titled *Fake: My Life as a Rogue Trader* by David Bullen. It is a story told by one of the former chief traders in the Forex department of the National Australia Bank about the bank's $360 million foreign currency scandal. It is a fascinating book that relates how, at one point, the president of the bank had not placed the proper controls over what his Forex traders were doing and describes the calamity that resulted. Because of the lack of rules or oversight, a rogue group of Forex traders began to take huge financial positions in various currencies. As the market started to move against them, they began to make their own rules to try and protect the bank's equity. In time, they started adding to their losing positions in hopes that they could cost average down (which is the term used in a trading strategy where additional positions are taken in the same direction at lower prices from the original entry, in an attempt to average out your buying price). In the 1990's many stock and mutual fund managers used the same strategy and unfortunately the currencies kept moving in the wrong direction, and the traders kept breaking all their own rules, losing millions of dollars from clients' account with every movement.

Like any group of kids that find themselves in major trouble, the traders agreed to hide their misdeeds. However, as is usually the case with wrong-doing, one eventually will become so guilt ridden that the individual has to spill the beans, and this situation is no different. After finding themselves in trading positions that had created unrealized losses close to $360 million, one trader couldn't stand it any longer and admitted what they had done.

Of course, ASIC (Australian Securities and Investment Commission, the regulatory body for the Australian government) stepped in and demanded the bank liquidate all its losing positions immediately to the tune of well over $360 million in losses. At the beginning of the investigation, it was determined that no real crime was committed by the traders—they were just irresponsible. The shareholders of the bank immediately demanded that the bank president be fired because of his lack of control over the bank. As the investigation continued, many believed the only real crime committed was that of ASIC, which demanded the bank liquidate its positions. This was clearly unfortunate for the bank, because soon after all positions were liquidated and losses realized, all the currencies took off in the opposite direction. If the four rogue traders had maintained their silence and just held onto those positions for one more month, they would have recovered from all their unrealized losses and probably would have made millions for the bank. This would have turned the bank president into a hero instead of a fired zero! The reality of the market and the amazing part of this story is that rule breakers are just as necessary as rule makers, and in the end the disciplined trader who abides by the rules makes a profit.

I want you to think about this next question: "Who trades in the financial markets?"

Banks? No.
Pension plans? No.
Brokerage firms? No.
Investment firms? No.
Financial institutions? No.

Individuals trade in the financials markets—human beings with human thoughts, human feelings, human emotions, and human fears. Humans who represent the organizations listed above make multimillion-dollar financial decisions.

THE GAME

Here is how it works. Bulls and bears fight aggressively to make the market go their way. For the Forex market to trade, there must be someone buying and someone selling simultaneously. In other words, one trader must be a bull going long and one must be a bear going short. Both traders are adamant about their positions, despite the fact that they rely on extremely accurate information, often from the same sources. What is amazing is they are adamant about the market going in opposite directions. In the market, the bulls and bears have different characteristics, yet they want the same thing—they both want to make a profit!

Bulls and bears enter the market buying or selling in hopes that more bulls or bears will enter after them, giving the market what is called bullish or bearish strength—creating a greater rally or greater dip. If their counterparts step in, the market will begin to move in their direction. Take the bulls, for example. If you wanted to be a bull, you would enter the market and, if your analysis was right, more bulls would enter and the market would begin to rally and reach new highs, or what is called higher highs. Now, what I have discovered is, most of the time, after the bulls achieve a new high, frequently prices start to retrace, or fall back down.

I was in George, South Africa, working at one of our international offices one afternoon and had been tracking a high on the GBP, the British pound, for several months. I was in one of our trading rooms with about 20 other traders when I asked, "Anyone wanting to make some money today? Just watch and trade the GBP. The bulls are after a high from several years back and when they get near it and/or take it out and achieve a new high, turn to a 15-minute chart and keep your eyes open for an evening star, engulfing bearish candle or tweezer tops. The second one of them appears, go short!" Sure enough, the bulls made a new high, and, shortly after, a bearish candlestick formation appeared, and the market fell 200 pips in about 45 minutes. Needless to say, I did not have to buy dinner that night.

This information is critical when you trade. Think about it, if you are a bull and have taken a bullish position and are looking for a place to get out of the market, the best place to get out is right before the market makes a new high and the bulls score a new point. Why? If the market begins to dramatically retrace after a new high is achieved, the market will take back all the profit it gave you.

I've received countless phone calls from people telling me, "I know where to get in, but I don't know where to get out! After I enter a trade, I sit there like a greedy idiot thinking the market will keep going to the moon, when all of a sudden it starts coming back to where I got in and all of a sudden I have lost all my profit—it was simply taken back!"

Oh boy, do we pay the price for our ignorance! It never ceases to amaze me that gamblers are surprised when they lose. What did they expect? Most traders are like gamblers, hoping lady luck will come their way. Little do they realize that in the back of the casinos, there are Palacio rooms, where educated gamblers play. These rooms are for private gambling, for gamblers with gambling systems, who frequently walk away with hundreds of thousands of dollars by using a well-researched approach.

People lose when they trade from ignorance, allowing their emotions to guide their trading rather than logic, education and information.

HOW DO BULLS AND BEARS SCORE POINTS?

Believe it or not, it is quite simple. Have you ever noticed that in life, the most obvious things are the hardest to see?

Bulls and bears keep track of all the previous highs and lows, no matter how far back they go. When bulls achieve a new high—higher than a previous high—they do what I call "scoring a point," and after the point is scored, the market pulls back. Conversely, the bears, too, are trying to score points by taking the market lower and making lower lows. When the bears make a lower low, lower than a previous low, they "score a point," which is followed by a pullback (see Figure 5-1).

Bulls and bears have memories like elephants; they never forget!

FIGURE 5-1   USD/JPY (Four-Hour Chart)

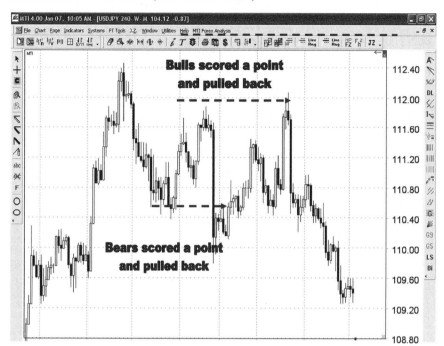

IDENTIFYING HIGHS AND LOWS

A high is visible as two candles to the left, two candles to the right that are lower than the center candle, and either the body or wick is higher. A low is visible as two candles to the left and two candles to the right that are higher than a center candle, and either the body or wick is lower (see Figure 5-2 (A–C)).

RESISTANCE AND SUPPORT

Bulls and bears play this eternal game 24 hours a day, seven days a week. Bulls fight for control, proving their strength by making new highs, and bears fight for the opposite.

As they make new highs and lows, levels of support and resistance are registered. The terms *support* and *resistance* were created back in the early 1900s in the stock market. *Support* occurs when traders begin buying, supporting a product, or stock, as it was falling. Conversely, *resistance* occurs

FIGURE 5-2

(A)
A high is different than finding resistance

- *__Highs__* are candlestick formations where there are 2 candles to the left and 2 candles to the right that are lower than the center wick high
- *__Current Resistance__* is a high that is lower than the previous high

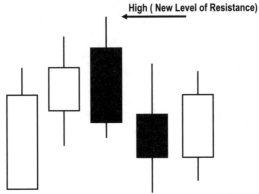

High (New Level of Resistance)

(B)
A low is different than finding support

- *__Lows__* are candlestick formations where there are 2 candles to the left and 2 candles to the right that are higher than the center wick low
- *__Current Support__* is a low that is higher than the previous low

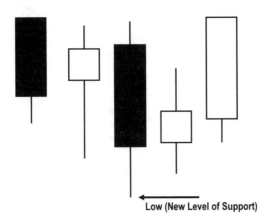

Low (New Level of Support)

FIGURE 5-2 *Continued*

(C)

when traders feel prices are getting too high or expensive and they resist buying at that price.

As traders supported a currency or stock at a certain price, a low or a new low in price was created for that product, and when they resisted buying, a new high was created for that currency. The game started when traders who were buying and selling tried to take prices still higher or lower. Buyers wanted prices to go lower so they could get a better deal, and sellers wanted prices higher to enable greater profits. This game of trading started shortly after Adam and Eve and has never ended. But it has just been within the past few hundred years that it has been captured and monitored in charts.

RESISTANCE

Resistance occurs when the bulls move the market to a new high that is higher than a previous high and the bears jump in aggressively selling, attracting more sellers than buyers, interrupting the rally and creating a retracement or pullback from that high. The new high becomes the new level of resistance, which is defined as a market high or a price level where bears start selling enough to interrupt and reverse a rally.

SUPPORT

Support occurs when bears move the market to a new low that is lower than
a previous low and the bulls jump in aggressively, buying to support the
price and attracting more buyers than sellers. That increased buying inter-
rupts the dip and creates a retracement or pullback from that low. The new
low becomes the new level of support, which is where bulls start buying
enough to interrupt and reverse a dip. Bulls on the Forex are the buyers who
are looking for opportunities to buy a currency pair at a low price in order
to sell it at a higher price for profit (see Figure 5-3).

The definition of the phrase "buy low, sell high" differs from one bull
to another.

"Buy low, sell high" to you may mean buying a product for $10.00 and
selling it for $15.00. I may buy the same product for $7.00 and sell it for
$30.00. Either way, we are both buying low and selling high. However, if
you do your transaction seven times a day, you will make $35.00 and would
be considered "scalping." I only need to do mine once to make $23.00 or
twice for $46.00, which is considered day trading. In the best of all possi-
ble scenarios, we would both buy right at the U-turn low and sell right at the

FIGURE 5-3   GBP/USD (Four-Hour Chart)

U-turn high, but rarely does it work that way. Most successful traders are more focused and more comfortable trading mid-way of a price swing, rather than going to extreme lows and highs in pursuit of profit.

As you read on, you will see I have pretty much figured out the *where* and *when* to enter the market, as well as the *why*—which is the logical and educational reason behind entering the market at this point. Knowing where the projected lows and highs will be will allow you as a trader to know when it is time to get in and get out of the market.

Bulls want to take the market to higher levels, enabling them to buy low and sell high. It is important to know how to identify those potential targets the bulls are aiming for. Past highs or major levels of resistance can be determined by looking at the current price and then working your way backward, as if you were climbing up a set of stairs (see Figure 5-4).

The major levels of resistance are the targets the bulls will be aiming for if they are in control or if they take back control from the bears. This happens when the market has reached a past level of resistance and established a new high. There are two reasons for a pullback, as seen in Figure 5-5.

FIGURE 5-4   USD/CHF (Four-Hour Chart)

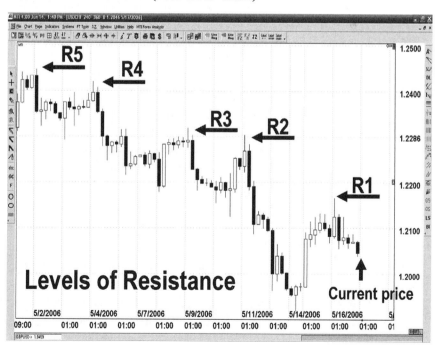

FIGURE 5-5   EUR/USD (Four-Hour Chart)

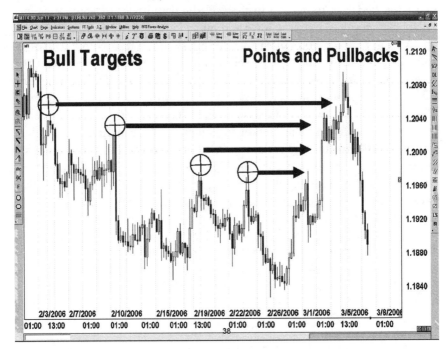

1. The first reason for a pullback could be the fact that traders that take short positions most of the time place their protective stop-loss orders near the last highs. This means that when the bulls hit that area, there is a lot of buy stop orders and a lot of selling—perhaps more selling than buying—taking place. Bulls succumb temporarily, bears start to gain a little territory, and a pullback or dip takes place. As a rule, prices will continue to fall until the bulls step in and support the price. Bulls normally support the price at one of three locations:

    - Near a past level of support
    - Near an uptrend line
    - At a Fibonacci up retracement number

    Sometimes all three are at the same numerical price point, which is then called a *convergence*.

2. The next reason for a pullback could be a Fibonacci up extension level. We will go into more detail about Fibonacci numbers in Chapter 8.

If the past level of resistance is penetrated and the uptrend is going to stay in place, the bulls will step in and start buying heavily near the last low or level of support. The first level of support becomes a great area to go long in the market, provided you get a bullish candlestick formation near a level of support.

LEARNING TO SHORT THE MARKET

Bears want to take the market to lower levels, enabling them to sell high and buy low, which is nothing more than buying low and selling high backwards. It is like your friend wanting to sell his house for what you think to be a good price.

He says, "I will sell you my house for $180,000. Anything you get over that, you get to keep." So you agree to buy his house at $180,000, providing you sell the house for more than you paid for it. The two of you agree that you get two months to sell the house before you have to actually buy it from him. As long as you sell it within two months for more than $180,000, you are going to make a profit. All of a sudden, you find a buyer at $220,000. Now you have to sell it to the buyer first before you buy it from your friend. In order to make your profit and earn your money, you now need to sell first at a higher price and buy second at a lower price. In the financial markets, this is called *shorting the market*, or *going short*, and having the market go your way.

Here is how you sell first, buy second, and have the market go against you. Let's say that during the two months you could not sell the house, and the market starts to crash. You panic because the house is now worth only $160,000 and still falling, yet you are under contract to buy it for $180,000. You decide to "dump it," or sell for $160,000 to avoid any further loss. So you sell it for $160,000, first, and then you buy it, second, at $180,000 and pay in the difference. This time the market did not go your way and you ended up buying high then selling low resulting in a loss of $20,000.

To avoid making losses, it is important to know how to identify those potential targets the bears are aiming for. Past lows or major levels of support are determined by looking at the current price and then working your way backward, as if you were walking down a set of stairs (see Figure 5-6).

The major levels of support are the targets the bears will be aiming for if they are in control or want to take back control from the bulls. This happens when the market reaches a past level of support and establishes a new low. There are two reasons for the pullback (see Figure 5-7).

FIGURE 5-6   USD/CHF (One-Hour Chart)

1. The first reason for a pullback could be the fact that traders that
    take long positions most of the time place their protective stop-loss
    orders near or at the last lows, meaning that when the bears hit that
    price point, there are a lot of sell-stop orders and a tremendous
    amount of buying taking place, perhaps more buying than selling.
    Bears succumb temporarily and bulls start to gain a little territory,
    and a pullback and small rally takes place. As a rule, prices will
    continue to rally until the bears step in and start selling again and
    bulls begin to resist buying because of all the selling. Bulls resist
    buying and bears start selling at one of three locations in a
    downtrend:

    •   Near a past level of resistance

    •   Near a downtrend line

    •   At a Fibonacci down retracement number

    You may also find all three at the same numerical price point, which is
    then called a *convergence*.

FIGURE 5-7   USD/CHF (30-Minute Chart)

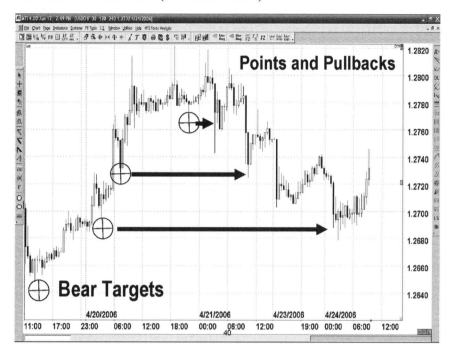

2.   A second reason for a pullback could be a Fibonacci down exten-
     sion level, which I will discuss in Chapter 8.

If the past level of support is penetrated and the downtrend is going to hold,
the bears will step in and start selling heavily near the last high or level of
resistance. The first level of resistance becomes a great area to go short
in the market, provided you get a bearish candlestick formation near
resistance.

PAST RESISTANCE CAN BECOME FUTURE SUPPORT

As bulls and bears continually play this wicked game of greed and
fear, bulls try to make higher highs and bears try to make lower lows. As
the market moves up, many times past resistance becomes future
support and becomes a great place to buy, but only after a bullish
candlestick formation appears at that most recent past level of resistance
(see Figure 5-8).

FIGURE 5-8   EUR/USD (One-Hour Chart)

PAST SUPPORT CAN BECOME FUTURE RESISTANCE

As the market moves down, many times past support becomes future resistance and becomes a great place to sell after a bearish candlestick formation appears at that most recent past level of support (see Figure 5-9).

VISUALLY OBSERVING THE GAME

Seeing is believing. In just about every MTI class around the world, we have our students experience the game firsthand, which is what you should do, too. Should you be unable to attend a MTI class, you can download a free seven-day trial of the MTI 4.0 charting package enabling you to watch the game firsthand.

Look at Figure 5-10 and study the chart closely. Look at the dates and times. Can you see all the past levels of resistance? Look how the bears have maintained control, making lower lows and lower highs. Bears have been scoring points, you just can't see them on this chart.

FIGURE 5-9   EUR/USD (Four-Hour Chart)

FIGURE 5-10   EUR/USD (Four-Hour Chart)

FIGURE 5-11   EUR/USD (Four-Hour Chart)

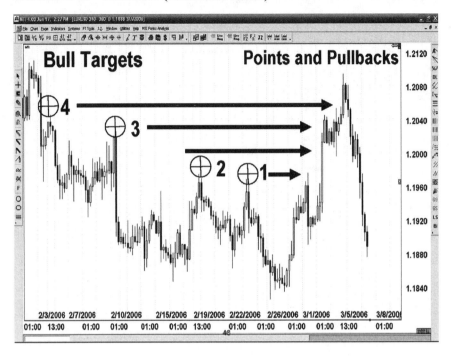

Now look closely at Figure 5-11. Here the bulls have taken control, reversed the market, and scored four points. After scoring the first point, there was a pullback. Points 2 and 3 were taken out by the same rally, followed by a small pullback. Point 4 was made with a small rally and a huge pullback. After the fourth level of past resistance was taken out by the bulls, the bulls could not sustain the rally to achieve a fifth point and the bears took control. You can clearly see that after the bulls scored the fourth point, the bears took control and reversed the market scoring two points or taking out the past two recent levels of support.

CONCLUSION

Trading is a game. It is a game played by two sides—bulls and bears—although there aren't actual bulls and bears, just human traders with very different opinions. They started out just like you and me, trying to figure out how this market works. Some have been washed out. Some are still surviving and trying to learn. Others have made it big, because they believed in their dream and stayed focused until they figured out what works. The way to learn how to win at this game is to work at it.

You have to move forward with the determination to succeed in this game. After all, the majority of work is done for you in this book. Experiencing success at trading will teach you how ultimately to succeed—you just need to take the time to understand truly what is written here.

Successful traders are successful for a reason. They take the time to educate themselves first about the opportunity, and then they calculate the risk versus the reward. With that calculated risk, they jeopardize their personal comfort level. A setback is an opportunity to start all over again more intelligently the second time around. Giving up along the way is the ultimate tragedy.

After teaching thousands of people how to trade, I would have to say the one personal characteristic I would regard as being the most important trait necessary to succeed at this game is the trait of persistence—the determination to endure to the very end after being knocked down 100 times, and getting back up a 101st time with a positive attitude. When you get to a point where you think this entire market, everything and everyone involved in it, is against you and you adamantly feel you cannot hang on, not for even one minute longer, it is right then and there that you cannot give up. This could be the place and time when everything turns around for you. The trader who can persist a little longer once his or her effort becomes painful is the trader who will find success at trading. For some reason, pain and suffering are our teachers and they help us persist until we can succeed.

True winners keep playing until they get good at the game and get it right. Our greatest achievement at trading is not in losing in a trade but in getting right back in there after something went wrong and we lost on a trade.

This game is not as hard as it looks. We make it hard. Successful traders will do what unsuccessful traders won't do. With their knowledge of how that market works, they create a clear trading strategy and a trading plan that they will follow with non-negotiable discipline.

Trading doesn't come natural for anybody. Learning to trade is not like learning a sport such as basketball or football. When it comes to trading, you get good by working hard and by practicing over and over again a trading technique that you understand. Success will come by not trying to do everything. You must keep it simple. *Do not* complicate it! When you make a mistake, remember, what doesn't destroy you will only make you a stronger and wiser trader.

TRENDS AND TRENDLINES

A TREND IS YOUR FRIEND

For some traders, learning to trade on the Forex is like learning how to build a car from scratch, without an instruction manual. Many of you have acquired quality parts, such as breaks, wheels, motors, seats, and steering wheels, yet as you attempt to put them together, you are not coming close to building that perfect little car you envisioned.

To become a successful trader, you need the right parts, with the right manual, to put all the parts together and have your car work properly. After all, a part such as a $2.00 gasket can bring your car to a screeching halt. Just look at what happened to the space shuttle *Challenger*.

I will never forget the day it happened. At the time, I owned a business that took photographs for NASA of all the work being done on the space shuttle at the Kennedy Space Center. We took pictures of all the different phases, from construction, to liftoff, to landing, and then had a company in Japan print laser photographs of the images for resale to the public. There were just as many employees who worked on the shuttle seeking these quality laser photoprints as there were tourists around the world wanting them. In fact, importing and exporting them is what introduced me to the exchange difference in currencies, which is how I became familiar with currency trading.

By 1986, laser photoprints had caught on and our company was offered licensee rights for many national parks around the United States, as well as for tourist parks such as Disney, SeaWorld, and Universal Studios.

Through our importing, we exchanged hundreds of thousands of U.S. dollars once or twice a week for Japanese yen. At the time, I really knew very little about currency trading, but I did recognize the constant fluctuation of the currencies as I was exchanging them. I wasn't trading the yen against the U.S. dollar to make money, but I saw that prices fluctuated up and down. So I watched the price movement to make sure I got the best deal at the time of the exchange; meaning, I was always waiting for the best time to make an exchange, enabling me to get as many yen as possible for my U.S. dollars.

In the late 1980s, I almost went bankrupt—not from mismanagement of my company, as the company was growing by leaps and bounds, but from the yen strengthening from 280 yen against the U.S. dollar to 150 yen to the U.S. dollar in less than 90 days. My cost of production doubled over a period of 90 days as the Japanese yen kept numerically falling and falling. The yen was increasing in value against the U.S. dollar as it dropped in price until it stabilized around 140 to 150 yen to the dollar. That is why products made from Japanese firms such as Sony and Sanyo doubled in price back in the late 1980s. That shift in economy opened the doors of opportunity for many U.S. manufacturers to now compete with the Japanese. It also forced the Japanese to start manufacturing their products here in the United States.

It is amazing how one person's loss becomes another person's windfall. I was going bankrupt, losing millions of dollars, while successful currency traders were making millions by shorting the market.

Had I taken the time to educate myself about currency trading and trends back then, using a simple piece of trading software like what we use at MTI, I could have been making $130,000 to $1,300,000 from a relatively small investment in the currency market, instead of losing millions as the U.S. and Japanese economies shifted.

I was unable to find a chart of the yen falling 13,000 pips back in the 1980s, however, I did find an example of a yen chart falling 3,100 pips in three months, between August 1998 and October 1998.

Looking at the chart of Figure 6-1, trading 10 lots or shorting the market with 10 lots by investing $10,000, brought a return to the trader of $300,000 in three months. Can you see how the inner trend line crossed over from the north to the south of the outer trend line, signaling a sell position for a long-term trader?

FIGURE 6-1   USD/JPY (Daily Chart)

TRADING A TREND UNTIL IT BENDS

Currency trading is very different than trading stocks. Companies can file bankruptcy, like Enron, or go completely out of business, taking their share value down to zero. On the other hand, with currency trading, there is no threat of a country going bankrupt. The country is not going to go bankrupt and turn the currency worthless. What *can* happen is that severe economic changes take place between countries, creating dramatic changes in the currency value of one country versus another. When that happens, it can create an incredible financial return for savvy, educated currency traders.

Study the four charts of Figure 6-2. In Figure 6-2A, the euro trended down 1,300 pips in four months, creating a $13,000 return trading one lot, or investing $1,000. How would you like to learn how to make this type of passive income trading long-term positions in currencies? A $10,000 investment would have brought a return of $130,000.

In Figure 6-2B, the Swiss franc (CHF) trended up 1,400 pips in four months, creating approximately a $13,000 return trading one lot, or investing

FIGURE 6-2   Identifying Trend Direction on Different Currency Pairs

(A)

EUR/USD (Daily Chart)

(B)

USD/CHF (Daily Chart)

FIGURE 6-2 *Continued*

(C)
GBP/USD (Daily Chart)

(D)
USD/CAD (Daily Chart)

$1,000. The reason is that the CHF does not pay $10 per pip—it has a fluctuating pip value.

In Figure 6-2C, the British pound (GBP) trended down 1,600 pips in four months, creating approximately a $16,000 return trading one lot, or investing $1,000.

In Figure 6-2D, the Canadian dollar (CAD) traded against the U.S. dollar (USD) and trended down 2,400 pips in seven months, creating a return of approximately $19,000 if you were trading one lot, or investing $1,000. The CAD also has a fluctuating pip value.

Trends appear across all time frames. They appear on monthly, weekly, and daily charts for long-term trading; they appear from eight-hour charts down to one-hour charts for day trading; and even on one-hour down to three- to five-minute charts for scalping.

Learning how to spot a trend that can last several hours for scalping, several days for day trading, and several months for long-term trading can create an enormous financial return for the skilled and educated trader.

The Forex trades 24 hours a day, and any time during those 24 hours you can turn on your computer and sit down to trade. The most important first step of success in trading currencies is determining market direction. The fact is if you want to make money currency trading, you will have to take a bullish or bearish position. One or the other—never both! You cannot make money taking a bullish *and* bearish position at the same time; you would be in a net zero position, making and losing the same amount of money with every pip movement.

People trade according to their personalities. Aggressive people love to scalp, while passive people prefer long-term trading. Figuring out your trading style is very important before you trade. However, whether you are a passive trader or an aggressive trader, you need to be able to determine market direction before you trade. You need to learn how to find the current trend before you enter the market, because you need to trade in the direction of the trend at all times. Do not fight the trend. Fighting a trend is like trying to swim upstream through violent forceful rapids. It doesn't work. Traders can make many mistakes. The biggest mistake is trading in the wrong direction!

One of the best ways to determine market direction is to have a piece of trading software, such as MTI 4.0, with an automated trend indicator that keeps up with the trend direction on any time frames (see Figure 6-3). As the market moves, the trend lines move with it. You can see how the market is constantly bouncing off the inner trend line. For example, on April 12, 2005, if the uptrend is going to stay in place when the inner trend line is broken, the market moves to the outer trend line and that is where the next

FIGURE 6-3   USD/CHF (Daily Chart)

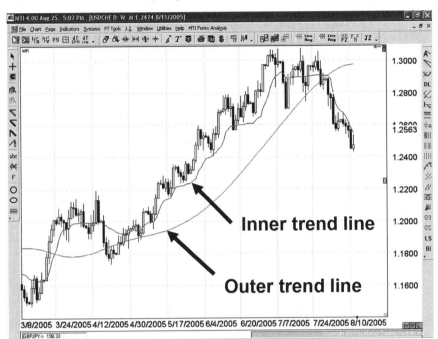

bounce will take place. It is when the outer trend line is broken that the majority of the time the market incurs a major reversal, as you see taking place around August 1, 2005, in Figure 6-3.

If you are an active trader and you use trading software that does not have a moving trend line indicator, you will need to learn the skill of drawing correct trend lines—with correct being the operative word. An incorrectly drawn trend line can mean the difference between making and losing money on a trade. Drawing trend lines is a skill that can be taught, but I think it is always best to have an automated trend line indicated on your software to keep up constantly with the trends you want to monitor.

In this chapter, we focus on finding, drawing, and monitoring three trend lines:

1. An inner trend line

2. An outer trend line

3. A long-term trend line

These Three trend lines form on all time frames and in both uptrends and downtrends (see Figure 6-4).

FIGURE 6-4

Drawing Uptrend Lines

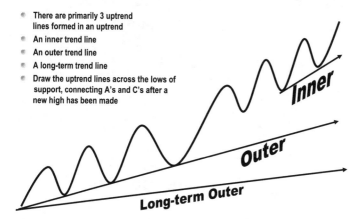

- There are primarily 3 uptrend lines formed in an uptrend
- An inner trend line
- An outer trend line
- A long-term trend line
- Draw the uptrend lines across the lows of support, connecting A's and C's after a new high has been made

Copyright 2005 by Market Traders Institute, Inc.

As the market moves, it will only move in one of three directions: up, down, or sideways. When it moves in any direction, it waves. Those waves become the emotional enemy of most traders. For some traders, it can take years to trust those waves and ride them to their end target.

SPOTTING AN UPTREND

If the market is going to move up, or trend up, on any time frame, it will wave up, creating higher highs, then wave back down, creating higher lows. I have never seen it go directly to the moon like an Apollo rocket. If it were to go to the moon, it would wave as it went, creating higher highs and higher lows. At some point, the trend will end, but until it ends, most successful traders try to take advantage of the move and take the ride up until it bends or ends. Believe it or not, most traders make all their money in trends and lose it all again in consolidation.

As the market trends in any direction, it moves at different speeds, just like a car. Most trends travel at a 45-degree angle as they move, akin to a car driving at normal speed. The trend line that is used for that 45-degree movement is called the outer trend. When a trend moves at a slower pace, a long-term trend line is created. Every now and then, the trend gets on a freeway at highway speed, ascending at a greater angle than 45-degrees, creating what is called an aggressive trend, or the inner trend line. Up and down inner trends, outer trends, and long-term trends all develop at the same time on all time frames (see Figure 6-5).

DRAWING UPTREND LINES

In drawing any uptrend line, you will draw a straight line, connecting all your visible levels of support without penetrating the bodies or wicks of the candles (see Figure 6-6). I have found that drawing the uptrend lines across the wick lows is more accurate than drawing them across the lows of the candle bodies and allows the trader to project the exact place of the future bounce (see Figure 6-6).

There is something magical that takes place when the market hits a trend line. Most traders call it a phenomenon. You will appreciate this phenomenon when it is explained in Chapter 8.

The market is like a large, never-ending river filled with violent rapids as well as slow-moving, calm waters. The market goes where it wants, when it wants, and yet it is governed by a set of natural laws, just like a river

FIGURE 6-5 EUR/USD (Various Time Frames)

FIGURE 6-6   EUR/USD (One-Hour Chart)

is governed by gravity and obstacles in its path. As the market moves in a direction, it has a tendency to retrace back to a trend line as if it were being directed by gravity and obstacles. If any current trend is going to stay in place, once it retraces back to a trend line, the market will bounce in the direction of its previous trend, and the trend line will act as the obstacle that will change the direction of the current movement. In other words, correctly drawn trend lines can project future levels of potential support in an uptrend and future levels of resistance in a downtrend.

FINDING AND DRAWING INNER, OUTER, AND LONG-TERM UPTREND LINES

You find and draw inner uptrend lines by finding the last two levels of support and drawing the line from left to right. You find and draw the outer uptrend line by starting at the far left of the chart and moving to the right, connecting the majority of your lower levels of support with a straight line. In other words, you start at the left of the chart and find your lowest wick low. From there you draw a straight line at about a 45-degree angle up, finding the next or higher level of support. You then connect the two wick lows, or levels of support, with the uptrend line, without penetrating any candles on the chart. As long as the chart is making higher highs and higher lows, you stay below the lows of support (see Figure 6-7).

Find and draw the long-term trend line by either compressing the chart or going to a larger time frame, connecting your levels of support starting from the far left of the chart moving forward. Because inner and outer trend lines form on all time frames, you need to look at a daily chart, where if you happen to see an inner and an outer uptrend line, the inner uptrend line will represent the most recent up movement for that time frame. The outer uptrend line represents the up movement over the past couple of months. If you look at an hourly chart, the inner uptrend line represents the up price movement over the past few hours, whereas the outer uptrend line represents the up price movement over the past couple of days. It is always best to compress your charts in the time period you are looking at to find any additional outer trend lines, or the long-term trend line.

FIGURE 6-7   EUR/USD (Four-Hour Chart)

Successful traders constantly monitor all uptrend lines on all time frames. Why? The movement on smaller time frames will always respond to the trend lines on larger time frames. This means that if the market is retracing back down toward an uptrend line on a daily chart, that retracement on the daily chart may be a 200-pip retracement and will form a downtrend on a 60-minute chart. If you only look at the 60-minute chart to do your analysis, you will be in a strong downtrend and your bias will be bearish. You will probably enter the market bearish. However, the way Murphy's law works, you will be entering at the end of that 60-minute trend, because as soon as the market from the daily chart hits its up trend line, the 60-minute chart will reverse and begin to rally, and you will be sitting there scratching your head, losing money and wondering what happened.

Once again, the inner, outer, and long-term uptrend lines can be found on any chart and on any time frame. Outer trend lines represent the overall movement on the chart for that time frame, and the inner trend line represents the most recent movement for the time frame. As long as the market is above the outer uptrend line, there is an 80 percent chance the market will continue bullish. You must remember, uptrend lines act as future levels of support. They are like a floor, and when the market hits them, they usually bounce back up. If the inner trend line is broken, the market usually moves to the outer trend line and will bounce back up from there. If the market breaks the outer trend line, the market will predominately move to the long-term trend line and bounce back up from there. If the long-term trend line is broken, as a rule there will be a major reversal (see Figure 6-8).

INCORRECT WAYS OF DRAWING UPTREND LINES

Correctly drawing trend lines will be critical to your success and will help to prevent you from losing money.

On one of my many trips to South Africa, I flew down to Cape Town to meet with a gentleman named Joubert who owned a trading company that was struggling. All their traders were losing way more money than they were making.

As I walked around the room for the first time, looking at their trading screens, I saw screen after screen with nothing but incorrectly drawn trend lines. I said to myself "no wonder they are all losing money!"

As I continued to walk around the room, looking at their screens, I noticed different trading systems and I wondered what other things they were doing wrong that they thought they were doing right. I was still

FIGURE 6-8   EUR/USD (Daily Chart)

standing there when, all of a sudden, one trader yelled out: "Swiss is getting ready to hit an uptrend line, get ready to trade it!" I walked over and looked at his screen only to quickly see, like all the others, he had incorrectly drawn his uptrend line.

I said, "Short the Swiss." Surprised and shocked, everyone in the room looked at me as if I were crazy.

He said, "Swiss is hitting an uptrend line, why would you even think of shorting it? Swiss is still in an uptrend and getting ready to hit a level of support."

I calmly replied, "The uptrend is dead on the Swiss, it is not hitting an uptrend line, it has already broken the inner and outer uptrend lines and is now moving to the long-term uptrend line, which is about 150 pips away. I would go short on the Swiss."

He asked, "What is an inner, outer, and long-term trend line?"

I replied, "That is why I am here."

He said, "Well, I'm going long."

I looked at everyone and said, "I guess this will be a moment of truth then." Then I looked at the traders and said, "From the screens I can see you are all drawing trend lines incorrectly. But if you believe in your uptrend line, then trade it and go long and I will understand." Then I said, "Anyone wanting to make money on Swiss, go short for the next 125 to 150 pips, then reverse your position and go long for another major move up."

As I walked into Joubert's office I held my breath, hoping that the market would continue to fall as I had predicted, knowing full well that the market does what it wants to do. Fortunately, Swiss fell exactly 150 pips to the long-term uptrend line and bounced back up like a basketball.

Trend lines need to be drawn correctly in order to make money trading. Learning the simple skill of correctly drawing trend lines can help you learn where to get in and can help you learn how to preserve your equity by getting out when it begins to turn. The following charts show the wrong ways to draw uptrend lines. In Figure 6-9, you cannot draw your uptrend lines through the candles of support—they must be at the bottom wicks of support.

FIGURE 6-9   EUR/USD (Daily Chart)

In Figure 6-10, the dotted line was at one point the correct uptrend line, but the market broke the uptrend line and retraced, continuing in an uptrend. As long as the market is making higher highs and higher lows, you cannot draw the line through the candles—you must draw the uptrend line across the lows of support.

In Figure 6-11, the uptrend is over and has been broken. The market is reversing and is currently trending down creating lower lows and lower highs. In this case, with the market creating lower lows and lower highs, you need to draw the uptrend line across the lows of support, until the market quits making higher highs and higher lows. The moment the market stops making higher highs and higher lows and starts making lower lows and lower highs, that is the moment the market is reversing.

Figure 6-12 shows that your trend lines must always be straight; they cannot be crooked. Only automated trend lines from your computer can wave or be crooked.

FIGURE 6-10   EUR/USD (One-Hour Chart)

FIGURE 6-11   EUR/USD (15-Minute Chart)

FIGURE 6-12   EUR/USD (One-Hour Chart)

FINDING AND DRAWING DOWNTREND LINES

One of the neatest things about learning to trade in this market is that in a downtrend, the market reacts the same way as an uptrend, but in the opposite direction. That means all the rules are the same, but in the opposite direction. Instead of the market making higher highs and higher lows as it trends up, it makes lower lows and lower highs as it trends down. Instead of the market bouncing up off an uptrend line, which is a future level of support, the market bounces down on a downtrend line, creating a level of resistance. Downtrend lines act as ceilings for the market and are future projected levels of resistance.

Once again, the best way to determine market direction is to start drawing trend lines. If the candles are above the uptrend line, the market is probably going to continue up. If the candles are below the downtrend line, the market is probably going to continue to trend down. Drawing downtrend lines is a skill that just about anyone can learn.

At the risk of repeating myself, the rules for drawing downtrend lines are exactly the same as drawing in an uptrend, but in the opposite direction. It is like turning everything upside down. Instead of drawing the lines across the lows of support we will draw the lines across the highs of resistance (see Figure 6-13).

FIGURE 6-13

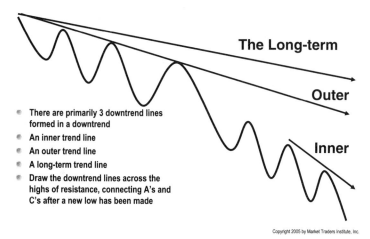

Drawing Downtrend Lines

The Long-term

Outer

Inner

- There are primarily 3 downtrend lines formed in a downtrend
- An inner trend line
- An outer trend line
- A long-term trend line
- Draw the downtrend lines across the highs of resistance, connecting A's and C's after a new low has been made

FINDING AND DRAWING INNER, OUTER, AND LONG-TERM DOWNTREND LINES

You find and draw the inner downtrend line by finding the last two levels of resistance and drawing the line from left to right. You find and draw the outer downtrend line by starting at the far left of the chart and moving to the right, connecting the majority of your higher levels of resistance using a straight line. In other words, you start at the left of the chart and find the highest wick high and, from there, you draw a straight line at about a 45-degree angle down, finding the next or lower level of resistance. You then connect the two wick highs or levels of resistance with the downtrend line, without penetrating any candles on the chart, following the lower lows and lower highs. As long as the chart is making lower lows and lower highs, you will stay above the highs of resistance (see Figure 6-14).

Now find and draw the long-term downtrend line by either compressing the chart or going to a larger time frame, connecting the levels of resistance starting at the far left of the chart moving downward. Because inner and outer

FIGURE 6-14   EUR/USD (One-Hour Chart)

trend lines form on all time frames, if you look at a daily chart and happen to see an inner and an outer downtrend line, the inner downtrend line will represent the most recent down movement for that time frame, or the movement over the past few days. The outer downtrend line will represent the down movement over the past couple of months. If you are looking at an hourly chart, the inner downtrend line will represent the down price movement over the past few hours, and the outer downtrend line may represent the down price movement over the past couple of days. It is always best to compress your charts in the time period you are looking at to find any additional outer downtrend lines or any long-term uptrend or downtrend lines.

Successful traders are constantly aware and monitor all trend lines on all time frames because the movement on smaller time frames will always respond to the trend lines on larger time frames. For example, if the market is retracing back up toward a downtrend line on a daily chart, that retracement on the daily chart may be a 200-pip move up. A 200-pip retracement from a daily chart will be an uptrend on a 60-minute chart. If you only look at the 60-minute chart to do your analysis, you will be in a strong uptrend and your bias will be bullish. You will probably enter the market bullish, however, the way Murphy's law works, you will be entering at the end of that 60-minute trend, because as soon as the market from the daily chart hits its trend line, the 60-minute chart will reverse and begin to dip, and you will lose money.

Just like uptrend lines, the inner, outer, and long-term downtrend lines can be found on any chart and on any time frame (see Figure 6-15).

Outer downtrend lines represent the overall movement on the chart for that time frame, and the inner trend line represents the most recent movement on that time frame. As long as the market is below the outer downtrend line, there is an 80 percent chance the market will continue bearish. Downtrend lines act as ceilings and future levels of resistance. If the inner downtrend line is broken, the market usually moves to the outer downtrend line and will bounce back down from there. If the market breaks the outer downtrend line, the market will generally move to the long-term downtrend line and bounce back down from there. If the long-term trend line is broken, as a rule there will be a major reversal (see Figure 6-16).

INCORRECT WAYS OF DRAWING DOWNTREND LINES

The same rules apply to drawing incorrect downtrend lines as they do to drawing incorrect uptrend lines, but in the opposite direction. Traders need

FIGURE 6-15   USD/CHF (Various Time Frames)

FIGURE 6-16   GBP/USD (One-Hour Chart)

to learn how to draw downtrend lines correctly in order to help them project the next bounce down. When you draw downtrend lines, you cannot draw your lines through the candles of resistance—they must be at the tops of the wicks of resistance.

As long as the market is making lower lows and lower highs, you cannot draw the line through the candles—you must attach the downtrend line across the highs of resistance.

The downtrend is over when the market stops making lower lows and lower highs and begins making higher highs and higher lows. When that happens, an inner, outer, or long-term downtrend line has been broken. As a rule, the market will begin to reverse in the opposite direction.

TRENDS INSIDE OF TRENDS

As the market moves, it can create trends inside of trends (see Figure 6-17). In this chart, you see the market aggressively trending up on the north

FIGURE 6-17   EUR/USD (Daily Chart)

side of the outer uptrend line, then breaking the inner uptrend line and reversing. After it reverses, it trends back down, forming the inner down-trend line until it hits the outer uptrend line, where it bounces and begins to trend back up forming an inner uptrend line again.

TRADING CHANNELS

As a trend moves, it likes to move inside a trading channel. A trading chan-nel is described as the market moving at an up or down angle inside two trend lines that create somewhat of a channel. The trend lines of the trading channels act as both resistance and support. If any are moving up—or a downtrend breaks a trend line and it stays in place—the trading channel will usually shift. In Figure 6-18, you see how a trading channel has shifted and how the centre uptrend line at one time was support for the market and with the shifting of the trading channel, now became resistance for the market in the new trading channel.

FIGURE 6-18   EUR/USD (Daily Chart)

THE VALUE OF TREND LINES

Using trend lines as part of your trading system, and in conjunction with other indicators, increases your chances of success. Why? Because of convergence, where there are several things taking place at a single price point, having several indicators could confirm and support trading decisions.

CONCLUSION

Uptrend and downtrend lines not only indicate market direction but also act as levels of support and resistance. In a downtrend, trend lines are future locations where the market may bounce back down. In an uptrend, trend lines are future locations where the market may bounce back up. Either way, they are just another little piece of the puzzle that increases the probability of a continued move. The key is to always look for that convergence, along with a trend line bounce in the direction of a trend.

The following are always great tools to use when determining when to enter this market:

1.   Trading software that can help determine trend direction with use of buy and sell signals
2.   Bullish and bearish candlestick formations
3.   Finding levels of support and resistance
4.   The knowledge that past resistance many times becomes future support, and vice versa
5.   The knowledge that trend lines act as floors of support and ceilings of resistance in the market and become visible locations for the next bounce in the direction of the trend

The more information you can gather as to why the market should bounce in a certain direction at a certain price point, the higher the probability for success. You now have five great trading tools to add to your tool kit, with more to come in future chapters. Regardless of how great a trade may look, it will always come down to trading within the equity management rules, which you will be learning about in Chapter 12. Even if you found a convergence with 15 reasons why the market should bounce in your direction, if the trade does not meet the equity management requirements, you need to have the discipline to pass on the trade. Trading will always be about risk versus your reward, just like life is.

7

BUY AND SELL ZONES

I T WAS **1984,** the space shuttle was getting ready to lift off, and the Kennedy Space Center called us up placing a laser photoprint order for well over $100,000. It was the largest single order I had ever received in my business career to date. I was so excited, I felt like I had just won the lottery. Proud as a peacock, I called my friend Brad Wagner and told him I had acquired VIP passes for the liftoff and wanted him to come down and join me for this memorable event. The VIP section sits only three miles from the launchpad, and when that shuttle lifted off, I have to admit, it was one of the most awesome and amazing events I have ever witnessed in my life. The sheer fact that people have been able to figure out how to get that much weight off the ground is beyond my comprehension, not to mention that even three miles away, when that shuttle starts to lift off, you can feel the ground shake as if you were in an earthquake and the air crackles like a diamond cutting glass.

Brad was twice my age, twice as smart, and a thousand times wealthier. He was in construction and had done very well. I met him when I lived in Hawaii, and we hit it off immediately. He was extremely smart, wise, and financially successful. He not only had one of the most beautiful homes in Hawaii, he also had several homes throughout America. We stayed in touch with each other through the years, and I considered him one of my mentors.

My real motive for inviting him to the liftoff was that I wanted him to see how I, too, was on my way to becoming successful—just like him. In addition to being a mentor, he was more like a second dad to me. He knew me when I was struggling to make ends meet and, for some reason, he took me under his wing without judgment, constantly mentored me, and told me I reminded him of himself when he was my age.

The day before liftoff, I took him with me in one of the company vehicles to deliver that $100,000 order. As we got in the vehcile to deliver the prints, I didn't mention a word about the amount of the invoice. I wanted to wait and let him see the amount as we were checking it in. He was shocked at the amount of the order. After we left, he said, "$100,000 is a lot of money! Wow, you are doing great for your age!" Back then, $100,000 *was* a lot of money and I *was* doing great for my age. What you learn with time is that it is all relative. As the saying goes, "A billion dollars isn't what it used to be."

I will never forget our ride back to the office. We came up to a toll booth requiring a $1.00 payment, and I reached in my wallet and pulled out a handfull of hundreds and gave one to the booth attendant. The attendant asked, "Do you have anything smaller?"

I said, "No."

Then he said, "Does your friend have anything smaller?"

Brad reached into his pocket and gave me a dollar bill and I paid the attendant. As we drove off, Brad looked at me and said, "One of the most valuable lessons you need to learn in your life is nothing lasts forever."

I quickly responded, "What do you mean?"

He continued, "You see that wallet full of hundreds?"

"Yes," I told him.

"Any fool can make money, but it takes a wise person to hold onto it. Believe it or not, I wake up every day fighting to hold onto what I have. The bigger question is . . ." and he paused, looked me in the eyes, and said, "how long will you be able to hold onto what you have acquired so far?"

I wasn't sure how to respond, I was caught between a wall of arrogance and a wall of ignorance and felt I had better take the humility door to get out. So I responded saying, "I don't know, I was hoping you could help and teach me."

He said, "Look at the sky. Today it's sunny, tomorrow it may be cloudy. Today you're happy and on top of the world with all those hundreds in your pocket, but perhaps something will happen over the next few days that will frustrate you and require you to use all those hundreds." Then he repeated what he said, "Just remember, *nothing lasts forever.*"

What he said next was equally important, but it didn't sink in until 10 years later.

He continued, "Because nothing lasts forever, as things start to change from good to bad, or from bad to good, nature will be fair and there will always be signs that you will need to pay attention to. Those signs will give you a heads-up of the change that is getting ready to take place. If you pay attention to those signs, you can begin to make the necessary adjustments to either hold onto what you are about to lose or aggressively start taking advantage of getting out of the mess you are in." Truer words were never spoken.

As you learn to trade, you must remember "nothing lasts forever." The fun and exciting times from learning to trade don't last forever, and the frustrating bad times from not paying attention and taking losses will not last either. Trends that start to take off and provide massive profits will not last forever. They all come to an end, but what is important is to look for the signs that can provide you with a heads-up of the end of a trend.

TRENDS

Forex trading is a financial game that is played 24 hours a day between the bulls and the bears. It is a perpetual war where the bulls and the bears each fight for control. As they fight for that control, they move in trends—uptrends and downtrends.

If the candles are above the outer uptrend line, the bulls are in control and have an 80 percent chance of maintaining it. If the candles are below the outer downtrend line, the bears are in control and have an 80 percent chance of staying in control. However, neither side will maintain control forever. When the market decides to increase its speed up or down, it moves above or below an inner trend line.

This fight for control goes on 24 hours a day, 5 days a week. It is an amazing game to watch and a crazy environment in which to make a living. In order to make money, however, you have to pick a side and take a position. You enter the market and get involved with something that is totally out of your control. In order to make a consistent profit, you need to learn the skill of properly tracking who is in control, which allows you to pick a bullish or a bearish side.

Fortunately, with the click of a mouse, you can switch teams anytime 24 hours a day, as many times as you like. There are pips and profit to be made on both sides and no one will think you are a traitor if you are a bull in the morning, a bear in the afternoon, and a bull again at night.

If you are trading in any direction and the market is trending, as long as it continues to trend in the direction in which you are trading, it is your friend. Why is it your friend? Because you are making money. The minute it starts to penetrate the trend line is the moment you need to remember what my friend and mentor Brad said: "nothing lasts forever." Start paying attention to the signs and recognize that this trend may soon be coming to an end. Then you need to start to tighten up your stops in order to protect the profits you have made and hold onto what you have.

Figure 7-1 shows how the euro 60-minute chart has been trending up, bouncing off of the uptrend line. It also demonstrates what a breaking of the trend line looks like. The bulls are losing their market strength and the bears are taking over by breaking the trend line.

As the control of the market shifts from bullish to bearish, or vice versa, trend lines get broken. If you were bullish in this chart and you were still holding onto your position as the market shift, the market would start to take back all the profits it gave you.

FIGURE 7-1   EUR/USD (One-Hour Chart)

BUY AND SELL ZONES

Trend lines divide buy zones from sell zones. A *buy zone* is the space above a trend line, whereas a *sell zone* is the space below a trend line—up or down (see Figure 7-2).

When the market is trading above any trend line, it is in the buy zone and traders are looking for the best location to buy the market. When the market is below the trend line, traders are looking for the best location to short the market. If a trader is long and the market starts to break a trend line, be it an inner, outer, or long-term trend line, the trader might consider getting out or reversing his or her position. If a trader is looking at the market going long and is waiting for the market to reverse, the best place to start to consider going short is after the market has broken the uptrend line and enters into the sell zone, as seen in Figure 7-1.

THE SELL ZONE

To help you recognize the signs to look for at the end of a trend, I want to go through the process step-by-step as it enters the sell zone. Figure 7-3 (graphical illustration) and Figure 7-1 (the actual market) show how a

FIGURE 7-2

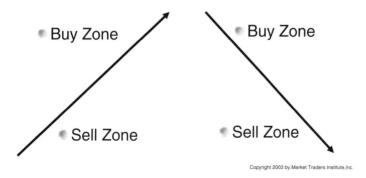

Trend Lines Divide Buy Zones from Sell Zones

Copyright 2003 by.Market Traders Institute,Inc.

FIGURE 7-3

When the market enters the
SELL ZONE...

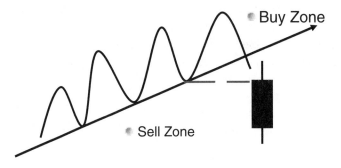

bearish candle has entered into the sell zone. But it is important to know that as the market enters into the sell zone, if a bullish candle appears immediately at the breaking of the trend line, instead of a bearish candle, the market is still potentially bullish. Furthermore, if a bullish candlestick formation appears shortly after the market enters into the sell zone, there is a high probability that the market is still in an uptrend and the trading channel may be shifting.

A very important sign to consider when the market is breaking a trend line is the angle of the trend line (see Figure 7-4). Traders think and act in probabilities and percentages, constantly monitoring high probabilities or high percentages against low probabilities or low percentages. When a trend line is penetrated and the market enters into a buy or sell zone, the angle of the trend line many times determines whether or not the market will reverse.

When the market breaks the uptrend line and enters into the sell zone, always take the time to check the angle of the trend line. The backside of the uptrend line will now act as resistance. Should the market begin to rally again, it will need to break through the backside of that trend line or resistance. If the backside of the trend line is lower than the last high, there is an 80 percent chance of a continued dip and a trend reversal. If the backside of the trend line is higher than the last high, there is an 80 percent

FIGURE 7-4

The angle of the trend line may determine the probability of the reversal

Copyright 2005 by.Market Traders Institute,Inc

chance of a continued rally. As time moves, it moves up and resistance moves with it. If it is higher than the last high, there is strong potential of a continued rally, and there may be an uptrend shifting of the trading channel as seen in Figure 7-6, but if it is lower than the last high, there is a good chance of a fall (see Figure 7-5).

As the channel shifts, the buy and sell zones shift as well. The market now enters into the sell zone of the old uptrend line and enters into the buy zone of the new uptrend line. Just because the market enters into the sell zone doesn't mean the trend is dead. In Chapter 6, you learned about inner and outer trend lines and that if the inner trend line is broken, the market predominately moves to the outer trend line and then bounces back up. The outer trend line is the one that carries the most weight in the market.

The strongest sign of a reversal, or that the uptrend is dead, is when the market retraces back to the latest level of major support. When the market breaks the outer uptrend line, the odds shift from 80 percent continued bullish to 60 percent continued bullish and 40 percent continued bearish. When the market returns to the major level of support, the market goes from 80 percent bullish to 80 percent bearish.

FIGURE 7-5   EUR/USD (Daily Chart)

FIGURE 7-6   USD/JPY (Four-Hour Chart)

SHORTING THE MARKET WHEN IT ENTERS THE SELL ZONE

Despite the probabilities and percentages the market gives you, remember that the market does what it wants when it wants—no matter what. The tools you currently have at your disposal to predict the market's next move include:

1. Trading indicators and systems
2. Candlestick formations
3. Support and resistance
4. Trends and trend lines
5. Buy and sell zones

Every trade involves risk and should be approached with proper equity management, which I will discuss in the coming chapters. If you want to short the market when it enters the sell zone, you must address your potential loss, should the trade not work out. I have always found that the best place to protect yourself financially, should the trade not work out, is by placing your protective stop-loss order above the last high of resistance, as seen in Figure 7-7.

FIGURE 7-7   USD/JPY (One-Hour Chart)

You do not want to risk much more than that, and you don't want to place yourself in a position to be hoping the market comes back. If the bulls take out the high, they will more than likely keep on going, taking out more highs as they play this game. There may even be a shifting of the uptrend channel, and you do not want to be trading against a trend. If the last high of resistance does not meet your equity management requirements, wait until the market rallies one last time and hits the backside of the uptrend line, as illustrated in Figure 7-7.

THE BUY ZONE

The buy zone works exactly the same as the sell zone, but in the opposite direction. Let me take you through the bending of a downtrend, step by step, to enable you to see how the market enters the buy zone. Figure 7-8 shows how a bullish candle has entered into the buy zone. It is imperative

FIGURE 7-8　USD/JPY (One-Hour Chart)

FIGURE 7-9

When the market enters the
BUY ZONE...

Buy Zone

that you understand that as the market enters the buy zone, if a bearish candle appears immediately at the break of the trend line (as seen in Figure 7-9), the market could still potentially be bearish.

A very important sign to consider is the angle of the trend line when the market is breaking a downtrend line as seen in Figure 7-10. When a trend line is penetrated and the market enters a buy or a sell zone, the angle of the trend line many times determines whether or not the market will reverse.

When the market breaks the downtrend line and enters into the buy zone, it is a good habit to check the angle of the trend line first. The backside of the downtrend line will now act as support. Try to determine if the market were to dip further at that moment in time, would the backside of the downtrend line be lower or higher than the last high? Should the market begin to dip again, it will need to break through the backside of that trend line of support. If the backside of the trend line is higher than the last low, there is an 80 percent chance of a reversal and new rally. If it is lower, there is an 80 percent chance of a continued dip, and perhaps a shifting in the trading channel. The backside of the downtrend line acts as support, and as time moves, it moves down and support moves with it. If it is lower than the last low, there is the high probability of a continued dip and there may be a downtrend shifting of the trading channel (see Figure 7-11). If it is lower

FIGURE 7-10

The angle of the trend line may determine the probability of the reversal

VS

FIGURE 7-11   USD/JPY (One-Hour Chart)

than the last high, there will be a high probability of a rally, as seen in Figure 7-12.

It is interesting to note that as the downtrend channel shifts, the buy and sell zones shift as well. The market now enters into the buy zone of the old downtrend line and enters into the sell zone of the new downtrend line. Just because the market enters into the buy zone doesn't mean the trend is dead. Don't forget that if the inner downtrend line is broken, the market predominately moves to the outer downtrend line and then bounces back down. The outer downtrend line is the one that carries the most weight in the market.

The strongest sign of a reversal, or that the downtrend is dead, is when the market retraces back to the latest level of major resistance. When the market breaks the outer downtrend line, the odds shift from 80 percent continued bearish to now 60 percent continued bearish and 40 percent continued bullish. It is when the market returns to the major level of resistance that the market goes from 80 percent bearish to now 80 percent bullish.

FIGURE 7-12   USD/JPY (One-Hour Chart)

FIGURE 7-13   USD/JPY (One-Hour Chart)

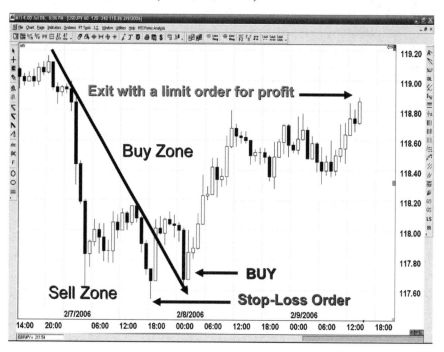

GOING LONG IN THE MARKET WHEN IT ENTERS THE BUY ZONE

When the market enters the buy zone, you will want to enter going long, placing a protective stop-loss order below the last low of support (see Figure 7-13).

CONCLUSION

Knowing about buy and sell zones can significantly aid your trading success; however, not all trend-line breaks offer trading opportunities. To become a good technical analyst, you need to be somewhat spatially intelligent—you need to be able to see things in a three-dimensional way and envision the future moves of the market. You need to keep in mind that the larger time frames control the movement of the smaller time frames. Not all trends are clear, and not all buy and sell zones are clear. So if the market is not clear to you, stay out.

It is amazing that common sense is really not that common. Be that as it may, you need to use your common sense when trading.

One summer I was working in our office in Johannesburg, South Africa. Behind our office is a beautiful park with a small stream and waterhole for children to play in. One day I arrived at work during a massive rainstorm. That gentle little stream behind the office had turned into roaring rapids, and the waterhole was now engulfed. I thought to myself, "wow, the water was crystal clear yesterday and today it looks extremely dangerous."

If that waterhole was your favorite place to swim, and you had made plans to go there after school with your friends but had found the muddy water and rapids when you arrived, would you still jump in? I would hope your common sense would tell you to stay out! The breaking of a trend line offers a tremendous amount of temptation to get in the market and go with the new trend. As a novice trader, don't use one single reason to get in—find as many reasons as you can.

When in doubt, stay out!

C H A P T E R

THE FIBONACCI SECRET

THIS CHAPTER IS EXTREMELY DEAR to my heart because knowledge of the Fibonaccis saved my financial life. You have no idea how many times I wanted to throw in the towel because I couldn't figure out how the market works. Every new trader has dreams, and those dreams can quickly turn into nightmares when you don't know what you are doing, which is why I am so adamant about finding a mentor. I didn't have a mentor, and my dreams quickly turned into nightmares.

The name Leonardo Fibonacci was airmailed to me straight from heaven. The understanding of his discoveries changed not only my trading career but also my life. What he discovered between the late 1100s and early 1200s explains how nature takes its course and proves that we are created in a numerical sequence, just like pinecones and pineapples. His discoveries also prove that the market is not this mysterious chaotic place that most people fear. It is a place where organized chaos exists, a dynamic system that is extremely sensitive to the human condition—the ebb and flow, the yin and yang, the action and reaction, the ups and downs of life. The Fibonacci Numerical Sequence is the ultimate display in the market of matter and energy and their interactions with each other.

When I heard about the Fibonacci numbers, back in the early 1990s, no one seemed to know anything about them. So I called my trading data provider, figuring that if anyone would know about the Fibonacci numerical sequence and how to trade it, they would. After all, they provide market data to more than 200,000 traders worldwide. To my surprise, the customer service representative had never heard of Fibonacci and suggested I talk to their programmer. Fortunately, he *had* heard of the Fibonacci retracement levels and asked if I wanted them programmed into the software. I was like a kid in a candy store getting free candy screaming, "Yes!"

As life goes, if it sounds too good to be true, it usually is. The next day, the programmer called telling me the Fibonacci retracement numbers were installed into the software. I told him, "Thanks a lot. Now can you show me how to use them in a trade?"

He was quick to respond, "No, I am just a programmer, not a trader."

I felt like I was ready to throw up from eating too much "false hope" candy from the candy store. I once again sat in disbelief that I was no better off today than yesterday and back at square one.

Things turn out best for those people who make the best of how things turn out. I figured that once I had the Fibonacci levels installed, I just needed to learn how to trade them. It looked like it was going to take a bit more effort than I initially anticipated.

So I started asking everyone I knew about the Fibonaccis again. A friend of mine told me about a new book by Larry Pesavento, *Fibonacci Numbers with Pattern Recognition*, which I raced out to buy.

As time went on, I established a cordial working relationship with Larry and soon recognized some fundamental differences in how the Fibonaccis should be traded in the market.

You can always tell who is the more experienced in any conversation. After everything is said and done, the wiser will always take the positions that they would rather be happy than right. So as we engaged in healthy discussion on how the Fibonaccis should be traded, Larry would always say, "Jared, if that way works for you, then I am happy for you and you need to keep doing that."

Learning how to trade the Fibonacci retracement and extension numbers like I do today started to make my life wonderful and successful. It became the main life preserver in my trading career as I moved forward.

THE HISTORY OF FIBONACCI

Leonardo de Pisa de Fibonacci, was born in 1170 in Italy and educated in North Africa, where his father, Guilielmo, held a diplomatic post. His father's job was to represent the merchants of the Republic of Pisa who were trading in Bugia, now called Bejaia (Bejaia is a Mediterranean port in northeastern Algeria), and Leonardo traveled with him, learning about math during his father's stay there. Little by little, he began to recognize the enormous advantages of the mathematical systems of the countries they were visiting versus the Roman numerals he had been taught.

One of the mathematical concepts that intrigued Fibonacci was the nine-digit system (1,2,3,4,5,6,7,8,9) used by the Indians.

Fibonacci's travels ended around 1200, and he returned to his hometown of Pisa. It was there that he started to work with the royal families, introducing the numbers 0 through 9 (a 10-digit system). It was there that he also wrote many of his texts, including *Liber Abaci* in 1202, *Practica Geometriae* in 1220, *Flos* in 1225, and *Liber quadratorum* in 1225. Producing a book during this time was a major task, given there were no typewriters or computers and everything had to be handwritten. For this reason, human civilization has unfortunately lost some of his works on arithmetic, such as Di minor guisa and his commentary on Euclid's elements. It is interesting to note that after Leonardo introduced 0, 1, 2, 3, 4, 5, 6, 7, 8, 9 to the Roman mathematical scholars, they debated for more than 300 years whether or not the number 0 was of any value.

Back in the 13th century, Europe predominately used Roman numerals for all its mathematical calculations. The problem is that it is virtually impossible to add, subtract, multiply, and divide using Roman numerals. And for that reason, historians could not quantify the wealth of a person. Think about it. How wealthy was King Solomon or King Harrod in Biblical times? No one knows. No one was able to quantify their wealth using Roman numerals. All we know today, via the Bible, is that they had more money than they needed or could spend. Today we can easily quantify a person's or company's wealth, so we know that Bill Gates is currently worth an estimated $56 billion, down quite a bit from $96 billion prior to September 11, 2001.

For those not familiar with Roman numerals, they are I = 1, V = 5, X = 10, L = 50, C = 100, D = 500, and M = 1,000. Fibonacci's claim to fame was the introduction of the numerical arithmetic system we know today: 0, 1, 2, 3, 4, 5, 6, 7, 8, 9. One of the most important books Fibonacci wrote was *Liber Abaci*, which means "The Book of Calculations" when translated. It was only after he wrote this book that the Roman numeral system was replaced by the Indians' nine digits and the Arabic *zaphirum* ("zero").

THE FIBONACCI NUMERICAL SEQUENCE

Fibonacci was fascinated with numbers, and his claim to fame was the discovery of a numerical sequence: the sum of the previous two numbers will always equal the next number in the sequence, as shown in the following examples:

$1 + 1 = \underline{2}$	$13 + 21 = \underline{34}$
$1 + 2 = \underline{3}$	$21 + 34 = \underline{55}$
$2 + 3 = \underline{5}$	$34 + 55 = \underline{89}$
$3 + 5 = \underline{8}$	$55 + 89 = \underline{144}$
$5 + 8 = \underline{13}$	$89 + 144 = \underline{233}$
$8 + 13 = \underline{21}$	$144 + 233 = \underline{377}$
	To infinity

THE FIBONACCI SEQUENCE IN NATURE

Since Leonardo's discovery, mathematicians have been fascinated with the relevance of this numerical sequence and ratios to our daily lives.

For example, mathematicians discovered the sequence in the breeding of rabbits (see Figure 8-1). If you start with one pair the first month, after two months you have two pairs. After three months you have three pairs, and this is where it starts to get interesting. You would think that they double each month, but they don't. After the fourth month, you only have five pairs. They multiply in the Fibonacci sequence.

FIGURE 8-1   Fibonacci Sequence in the Animal Kingdom

Sequences in Nature

Rabbits Breed In Numerical Sequence

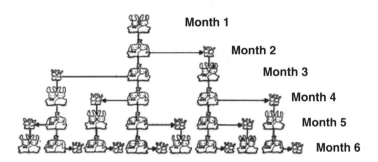

Month 1

Month 2

Month 3

Month 4

Month 5

Month 6

1-2-3-5-8-13-21-34-55-89...

What is terrifying is if rabbits were left alone to multiply in this sequence and keep going for only 100 months, the total number of pairs would be 354,224,848,179,261,915,075.

Figures 8-2 to 8-5 show how the Fibonacci numerical sequence plays out in nature.

FIGURE 8-2   Fibonacci Sequence in Nature

Pineapples Grow in a Numerical Sequence

8 parallel rows
of scales spiraling
gradually

13 parallel rows
of scales spiraling
at a medium slope

21 parallel rows
of scales spiraling
steeply

1-2-3-5-<u>8-13-21</u>-34-55-89...

FIGURE 8-3   Fibonacci Sequence in Horticulture (The Study of Flowers)

Sunflowers Grow in a Numerical Sequence

55 parallel rows of
seeds spiraling
counterclockwise

89 parallel rows of seeds
spiraling clockwise

1-2-3-5-8-13-21-34-<u>55-89</u>...

FIGURE 8-4   Fibonacci Sequence in Seed Growth

Pinecones Grow in a Numerical Sequence

13 parallel rows

8 parallel rows

1-2-3-5-<u>8-13</u>-21-34-55-89...

FIGURE 8-5   Fibonacci Sequence in Dendrology (The Study of Trees)

A Sneezewort Branch Grows in a Numerical Sequence

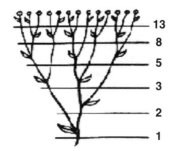

1-2-3-5-8-13-21-34-55-89...

The Fibonacci sequence exists in other areas of our lives, too.

For example, look at the piano. The piano of today took more than 300 years to perfect. Yet the actual construction of the piano, including its quantity of keys, has not changed since that time (see Figure 8-6).

When the conditions of life are so closely linked to nature, not much is left to human control. Believe it or not, the Fibonacci series of numbers is a lot more than just a source of amusement. Watch what happens when you start dividing the numbers:

> Take any three numbers in the numerical sequence after the first seven sets of numbers. Start dividing them and watch what happens.
>
> For example, let us take 144 + 233 = 377.
>
> If you divide the sum 377 by the first number of the sequence, 144, you will get a ratio of 2.618.
>
> If you divide 233 by 144, it will equal a ratio of 1.618.
>
> If you divide 144 by 233, it will equal a ratio of 0.618.
>
> If you divide 144 by 377, it will equal a ratio of 0.382.

It doesn't matter which numbers in the sequence you divide with each other, you will still come out to the Fibonacci ratios listed above.

One interesting aspect of the summation progression is that it doesn't matter where you start. Take any two numbers, like 5 and 100, and you will see the same aspects and series: 5 + 100 = 105, 100 + 105 = 205, 105 + 205 = 310,

FIGURE 8-6   Fibonacci Sequence in Music

A Piano's Octave Is in a Numerical Sequence

1 octave
2 black keys
3 black keys
5 total black keys
8 white keys
13 total keys per octave

1-2-3-5-8-13-21-34-55-89...

$205 + 310 = 515$, $310 + 515 = 825$, $515 + 825 = 1,340$, $825 + 1,340 = 2,165$, and so forth.

Now, start to divide these numbers and you will find the same ratios:

825 divided by 1,340   = 0.616 (which is close to 0.618).
1,340 divided by 2,165 = 0.618.
2,165 divided by 1,340 = 1.616 (which is close to 1.618).
1,340 divided by 825   = 1.624 (which is close to 1.618).

I show you these examples in the hope of turning you into a believer. After all, you need to believe in the Fibonacci numbers as you trade.

There are six sets of numbers that you need to know. They are

0.382
0.50
0.618
0.786
1.27
1.618

You are probably thinking, where do 0.50, 0.786, and 1.27 come from? The 0.50 comes from taking the sum of the three numbers and dividing them by 2. The 0.786 comes from the square root of 0.618, and the 1.27 comes from the square root of 1.618. All of these numbers are important in the market and relevant to our daily lives.

One of the reasons the pyramids in Egypt have stood the test of time is that the height of the pyramid divided by the length of the pyramid equals a Fibonacci number of 0.618 (see Figure 8-7).

Have you ever experienced goose bumps when you listen to music? Scientists have been able to prove that the reason you get those goose bumps is that two or more keys are being played and they vibrate in a Fibonacci numerical ratio sequence (see Figure 8-8). See how key C vibrates at 264 vibrations per second and key A vibrates at 427 vibrations per second. When you divide the vibrations of the key of C at 264 vibrations per second by the vibrations of the key of A at 427 vibrations per second, you get a Fibonacci ratio of 0.618.

The amazing fact about the composition of the human body is that it, too, is based on Fibonacci ratios. Don't believe it? Go grab a measuring tape and a calculator, because I am going to make a believer out of you.

First, measure your height in inches.

For example, let's say you are 5 feet 10 inches, which is 70 inches. Take 70 inches and multiply it by 0.618 using your calculator. You should get

FIGURE 8-7   **Fibonacci Sequence in Architecture**

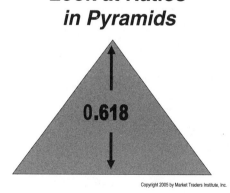

*Look at Ratios
in Pyramids*

0.618

FIGURE 8-8   Fibonacci Sequence in Harmonic Vibrations

A piano's keys vibrate at 0.618 ratios to other keys as it is played

- Key C vibrates at 264 vibrations per second
- Key A vibrates at 427 vibrations per second
- <u>264 divided by 427 = 0.618</u>

43.26 inches. Take your measuring tape and start at the ground moving up. At 43.26 inches, you will find your belly button. Take the distance from the top of your head to your belly button and multiply it by 1.618. That will be the distance from your belly button to the bottom of your feet (see Figure 8-9).

THE HUMAN FACE

Knowledge of Fibonacci ratios and rectangles goes back to the Greeks, who based their most famous work of art on them: the Parthenon is full of *golden rectangles*. Fibonacci studied the Greek mathematical ratios and through his discoveries standardized these ratios which later were commonly referred to as *Fibonacci ratios*. Followers of the Greek mathematician Pythagoras thought of the Fibonacci ratio as divine. And even today, the Fibonacci ratio is in human-made objects all around us. Look at almost 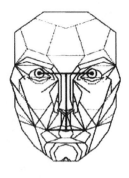 any Christian cross—the ratio of the vertical part to the horizontal is 0.618.

Despite these numerous appearances in works of art throughout the ages, there is an ongoing debate among psychologists about whether people really do perceive the golden shapes (which are objects that are visually balanced in a Fibonacci numerical sequence or ratio), particularly the

FIGURE 8-9   Fibonacci Sequence in the Human Body

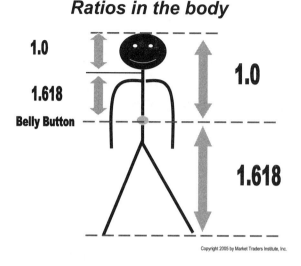

Ratios in the body

1.0

1.618

Belly Button

1.0

1.618

golden rectangle, as more beautiful than other shapes. In a 1995 article in the journal *Perception*, Professor Christopher Green of York University in Toronto, Canada, discusses several experiments that have shown no measurable preference for the golden rectangle, but notes that several others have provided evidence suggesting that such a preference exists.

Regardless of the science, the golden ratio (Fibonacci ratio) retains a mystery, partly because approximations of it turned up unexpectedly in nature.

The Discovery Channel had a televised special, "Fibonaccis in the Face," which was about a plastic surgeon who creates a face on computer using only Fibonacci ratios to place the eyes, eyebrows, ears, nose, mouth, and cheeks on the face. When he is done, he hits the print button and a mold of a beautiful face appears. He then takes several model magazines and scans the faces of males and females alike—people we think of as beautiful. After he does that, he places the mold he created over the mold of the models and it fits perfectly.

He then scans pictures of scary-looking people, such as those in horror movies, and creates molds of their faces. But when he places the mold he created over the mold of their ugly faces, it doesn't fit. The eyes are off-center, the nose is off-center, the cheek bones are too high or too low, and what he concludes is that the human eyes and mind use numbers to determine beauty. If the numbers are in a Fibonacci numerical sequence, we consider that person to be beautiful; if they are not, we consider them to be ugly. Figure 8-10 shows how some of the facial features are at Fibonacci numbers.

THE FIBONACCI RETRACEMENT AND EXTENSION RATIO RELATIONSHIP

The reason I have gone into such depth explaining the Fibonacci numbers is to provide you with a fundamental belief that they exist. They are real. But it is only when you understand and recognize the value of these numbers in your life that you will be able to believe and apply them in the financial markets with confidence.

Each ratio needs to be divided into two categories: a retracement number and an extension number. The following identifies which numbers are in which category:

Retracement Numbers	Extension Numbers
0.382	1.618
0.50	1.27
0.618	
0.786	

FIGURE 8-10   Fibonacci Sequence in the Human Face

Ratios in the Face

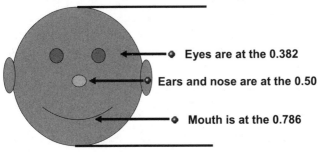

Eyes are at the 0.382

Ears and nose are at the 0.50

Mouth is at the 0.786

In an uptrend, the market is making higher highs and higher lows, and in a downtrend, the market is making lower lows and lower highs. The wave movements in both uptrends and downtrends move in an A, B, C, D formation. In an uptrend, the low or start of the rally is considered an A. After the rally tops out or the move comes to an end, that high is considered a B. As the market begins to retrace back inside the AB boundary, the end of the retracement low is considered a C, and the new rally, which rallies higher than the B and tops out, is called the D extension. In summary, as the market moves up, it moves in an up A, B, C, D, sequence—the initial rally—followed by a retracement, which again is followed by a new rally to the D extension.

In the up A, B, C, D sequence, after the B high is formed, the market retraces back down into the AB boundary, where the bulls and bears fight for control. The Fibonacci retracement levels act as future hidden levels of support. If the uptrend stays in place, it will be at one of these levels that the market will bounce back up. Many times that bounce back up will be near an uptrend line or a past level of resistance. If it does bounce there, that is called bouncing at a convergence.

As seen in Figure 8-11, the starting point A acts as point 0, and B acts as the end of the move. The move from A to B is considered 100 percent, or equals 100 percent of the initial move. As the market retraces, if it

FIGURE 8-11 Fibonacci Sequence in an Uptrend

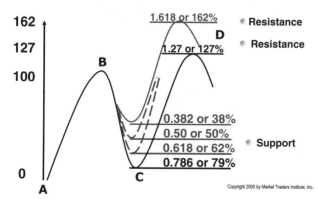

*Fibonacci ratios are hidden potential
levels of support and resistance*

U-turns or bounces back up at the 0.382, it means the market has come back 38 percent or 38 pips if the original AB move were 100 pips. If it retraces back to the 0.50, which is the halfway point, then it equals a 50-pip retracement if the initial move were 100 pips, and so on.

After the market bounces at a Fibonacci retracement number, U-turns, and rallies to the D extension number like the 1.27 level, it has moved 27 percent above the original AB move, or a total of 127 percent of the initial move. If it rallies to the 1.618, it has moved 62 percent above the original AB move, or a total of 162 percent of the original AB move (see Figure 8-11).

As the saying goes, "Tell me where the market has been, and I will tell you where it is going to go." Should the market bounce at the 0.382, 0.50, or 0.618, it will predominately rally and go to a 1.618 extension, which is considered D. If it retraces all the way down to the 0.786, it will only go to the 1.27 extension, as seen in Figure 8-12.

The opposite takes place in a downtrend. (If you are spatially challenged, imagine everything upside down). In Figures 8-13 and 8-14,

FIGURE 8-12   AUD/USD (One-Hour Chart)

FIGURE 8-13   Fibonacci Ratios in Support and Resistance

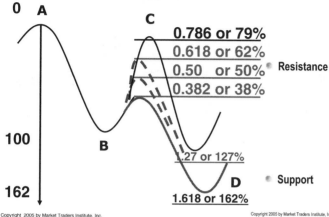

Fibonacci ratios are hidden potential levels of support and resistance

you can see that in a downtrend, the retracement ratios are potential hidden levels of resistance and the extensions are hidden levels of support.

Believe it or not, some trading programs do not have all the Fibonacci retracement levels and extensions. The MTI 4.0 trading software has the Fibonacci tool that becomes critical in analyzing your trade. As you use the Fibonacci trading tool in your trading software, always start by connecting the A to the B to find the retracement and extension ratio numbers. The settings in your software will automatically find the retracement and extension levels for you. In an uptrend, use your Fibonacci tool to connect point A and point B and find the retracement levels of support and the extension levels of resistance, as seen in Figure 8-11 and 8-12. In a downtrend, use your Fibonacci tools to connect point A and point B to find your retracement levels of resistance, as well as your extension levels of support, as seen in Figures 8-13 and 8-14.

When we discussed trend lines, I pointed out that the market moves at different speeds, forming inner and outer trend lines, just like cars move at different speeds in a neighborhood versus on the freeway. Now I am going to explain why: the speed of the market is usually dependent on where the U-turn is in the retracement, or at what Fibonacci retracement level the market bounced (see Figure 8-15).

FIGURE 8-14   AUD/USD (One-Hour Chart)

FIGURE 8-15   Fibonacci Ratios Determine Market Momentum

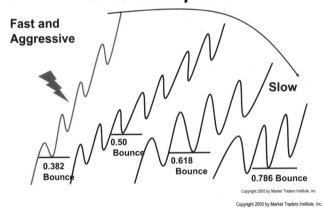

Copyright 2005 by Market Traders Institute, Inc.

Copyright 2005 by Market Traders Institute, Inc.

These rules apply to the movement in an uptrend as well as a downtrend.

THE 0.382/1.618 RATIO RELATIONSHIP

In an uptrend, as seen in Figure 8-15, when the market only retraces back to a 0.382, U-turns, and rallies, it is on the move. It is like a car traveling on a freeway—a sign of volatility and rapid movement. After the bounce, it will then usually rally beyond the 1.618 extension by about 15 to 20 percent before it bounces back down. In a downtrend, when the market only retraces back to a 0.382, U-turns, and dips, it, too, is on the move. It is also like a car traveling on a freeway and is a sign of volatility and rapid falling movement. After it bounces at the 0.382, it will then usually dip beyond the 1.618 extension by about 15 to 20 percent before it bounces back up.

THE 0.50/1.618 RATIO RELATIONSHIP

In an uptrend, as seen in Figure 8-15, when the market retraces back to the 0.50, U-turns, and rallies back up, it is slowing down a bit but is still on the move. It is like a car traveling 45 MPH in a business district. After the bounce, it will then usually rally to the 1.618 extension before it bounces back down. In a downtrend, when the market retraces back to the 0.50, U-turns, and begins to dip, it, too, is slowing down a bit but is still on the move. It will usually dip to the 1.618 extension before it bounces back up.

THE 0.618/1.618 RATIO RELATIONSHIP

In an uptrend, as seen in Figure 8-15, when the market retraces back to the 0.618, U-turns, and bounces back up, it is slowing down. It is like a car traveling 35 MPH in a congested business district. After the bounce, it will then usually rally to the 1.618 extension before it bounces back down. Because it is slowing down, it may even bounce at the 1.27 level of resistance first, creating a small a, b, c, d, between the C, D. In a downtrend, when the market retraces back to the 0.618, U-turns, and dips, it, too, is slowing down. It may bounce at the 1.27 extension of support first on its way to the 1.618 extension. When it hits the 1.618 extension of support, it will probably bounce back up.

THE 0.786/1.27 RATIO RELATIONSHIP

In an uptrend, as seen in Figure 8-15, when the market retraces back to the 0.786, U-turns, and bounces back up, it is really slowing down. The car has now entered into the neighborhood traveling at 25 MPH. After the bounce, it will only rally to the 1.27 extension before it bounces back down.

Because it is slowing down, it may first create a small a, b, c, d wave between the C, D. In a downtrend, when the market retraces back to the 0.786, U-turns, and dips, it, too, is slowing down, like a car traveling at 25 MPH. Because it is slowing down, it may first create a small a, b, c, d wave between the C, D after the bounce. It will only dip to the 1.27 extension of support before it bounces back up.

SMALL a, b, c, d's FORM INSIDE C, D's

Now that we know that the market moves at different speeds, we need to look a little deeper into that movement. If the distance between a C and a potential D is substantial, and there are no fundamental announcements, the market often forms small a, b, c, d's between the C, D. This is important to recognize because most traders are very impatient and want instant gratification. If a trader has entered the market long or buying, every time the market begins to retrace or dip, the trader starts to panic and is tempted to exit.

A good habit to get into is to envision the market movement before you execute the trade. Draw out how you envision the future wave will be. Try to figure out the amount of time you will need to be in that trade. Then decide to be a scalper, a day trader, or a long-term trader before you enter the market. This will keep you from getting frustrated and emotional as you trade. You must never forget the ebb and flow of the markets and that these markets wave. It is a natural wave. Very seldom will they race to your target, regardless of how much you want them to or how little time you have set aside for trading. The market moves at its own pace, not ours.

THE VALUE OF ADDING THE FIBONACCI NUMBERS TO YOUR TOOLBOX.

Let's put everything you have learned so far together to increase your percentage of finding a winning trade. The natural law of the Fibonacci numerical sequence is not capricious, it works on every time frame and in every market. It is just as valid in the Forex as it is in the stock or commodity markets. As a matter of fact, anywhere you can pull up a financial chart, on any time frame, you will see the Fibonaccis in action.

I will never forget one class I taught in Sydney, Australia, when I met an older gentleman, named John, who introduced himself to the class by stating: "I have come to take your course because three years ago, I bought $250,000 worth of Qantas stock at $2.00 a share. I told myself when it hits $5.00 a share, I'm selling." He proceeded, saying, "That #@*#@* stock went to $4.90 cents a share, looked at all my sell orders, laughed in my face, then U-turned and is now back around $2.00 a share. I came here to figure out what happened and why I was so greedy and didn't sell at $4.90 a share. That was my retirement money." This reminded me of a saying my dear friend and mentor Fred Gronbacher taught me, it goes something like this: "The ignorant must suffer."

I told John, and the class, "After I teach you how the markets work, on the last day of the class, we will pull up a chart and look at Qantas stock. Mark my words, and write this down right now." Everyone grabbed a piece of paper and started writing. "On Saturday, when we pull up the chart, at $4.90 there will be a bearish candlestick formation at a D Fibonacci extension level followed by an uptrend line break, the reversal will create a bearish 'king's crown,' and the market will begin to make down A, B, C, D all the way down to $2.00 a share." I would have showed all of them at that moment what I was talking about, but it would have been of no value until they finished the course.

After class on the third day, we pulled up a Qantas chart and, sure enough, right before everyone's eyes was one of the most beautiful evening stars at a D Fibonacci extension level. This was followed by an uptrendline break, a bearish king's crown, and down A, B, C, D's. John jumped up out of his seat as he was sitting on the first row and, in front of 45 people, grabbed me, gave me a bear hug, and kissed me on my cheek. The class began to laugh, but as John pulled away, he looked at me with a tear in his eye, whispering "Thank you, chief!"

It has been from countless moments like these, shared by great people like John, that I have found my true destiny in life. I have learned we make a living by what we get, but we make a life by what we give.

CONCLUSION

Knowing where to get into the market and where to get out, and why, is about as close to the holy grail that you'll ever get. Understanding that nature exists in the market, and how it works, places the trader at a huge advantage. It allows a trader to wait for the retracement bounce at a pre-projected retracement number, having the market move in their direction from entry, which is every trader's dream, then riding it to the preprojected corresponding Fibonacci extension.

As you read the step-by-step rules of trading a trend, try to envision the movement of the market and the trading process. This methodology works on all time frames and in all markets.

In life, the more we try to avoid financial suffering or any kind of suffering, the more we suffer because what we think is mysterious many times is nothing more than simple knowledge that needs to be understood. You need to learn to become financially empowered instead of financially vulnerable. Nothing I teach is to be feared, only understood. Have the courage to become empowered in Forex, only then will you be successful in trading Forex.

STEPS TO BE FOLLOWED WHEN TRADING AN UPTREND

1. Draw all uptrend lines and downtrend lines, inner, outer, and long-term. (This will help to determine if the market is in an uptrend, downtrend, or if a trend line has been broken, signifying the potential end of a trend or a reversal.)

2. Find the latest upward A, B and use the Fibonacci tool on your trading software to draw the Fibonacci retracement and extension lines.

3. Find a C buy-entry at a convergence, such as a Fibonacci retracement level, upward trend line, morning star, tweezer bottom, or bullish engulfing candle.

4. Find the projected Fibonacci D extension, as well as four levels of past resistance. Find the closest level of resistance to the Fibonacci extension. Place a limit exit order 10 pips in front of, or before it hits, either the Fibonacci extension or the level of resistance (remember when the bulls score a point it always pulls back).

5. Look at your potential financial risk with your protective stop-loss order. If you can't afford the potential loss should the trade not work out, then *stay out and do not trade!*

6. Pull out your trader's checklist that you have created or the one supplied by Market Traders Institute. Create a trading plan and trade your plan.

STEPS TO BE FOLLOWED WHEN TRADING A DOWNTREND

1. Draw all uptrend lines and downtrend lines, inner, outer, and long-term. (This will help to determine if the market is in an uptrend, downtrend, or if a trend line has been broken, signifying the potential end of a trend or a reversal.)

2. Find the latest downward A, B. Use the Fibonacci tool on your trading software to draw the Fibonacci retracement and extension lines.

3.   Find a C sell-entry at a convergence, such as a Fibonacci retrace-
     ment level, downward trend line, evening star, tweezer top, or
     bearish engulfing candle.

4.   Find the projected Fibonacci D extension, as well as four levels of
     past support. Find the closest level of support to the Fibonacci
     extension. Place a limit exit order 10 pips in front of, or before it
     hits, either the Fibonacci extension or level of support (remember
     when the bears score a point it always pulls back).

5.   Look at your potential financial risk with your protective stop-loss
     order. If you can't afford the potential loss should the trade not work
     out, then *stay out and do not trade!*

6.   Pull out your trader's checklist that you have created or the one sup-
     plied by Market Traders Institute. Create a trading plan and trade
     your plan.

Fibonacci numbers are really significant and play a big part in our
lives. Learning the Fibonacci numerical sequence and trading ratios adds a
very important tool to your trader's toolbox.

Many traders fail because they are too busy trying to tell the market
what to do. *Do not* try to tell the market what to do—that is like telling the
rapids to step aside because you want to leisurely swim upstream. It is not
going to happen. Learn how to read the markets. Let it tell you what it is
going to do and then go with it.

There is a reality as you trade, and you need to accept the fact that you
cannot make money 100 percent of the time in the market, even with the
knowledge of the Fibonaccis. But you can execute your trades 100 percent
of the time using productive trading rules and become a winning trader,
even by only winning 50 percent of the time, provided you maintain the
right equity management.

9

THE REALITY OF THE FIBONACCI SECRET

I WANT TO DEDICATE this chapter to all the families who lost loved ones in the September 11, 2001, tragedy, as well as the countless millions who were affected by that day.

FIBONACCI MARKET MOVEMENT ON SEPTEMBER 11, 2001

On September 11, I learned that adversity causes some men to break and even crumble, whereas others willingly rise to the occasion and break records. Americans, on that day and the days that followed, proved that difficulties are meant to rouse, not discourage.

I think back on how that day started. It was nothing but blue skies and another beautiful day in sunny Florida. As a matter of fact, the whole east coast of the United States was free of clouds. I was trading from my office at home, expecting an average non–fundamental trading day (see Chapter 10). I was trading the euro, the British pound, the Swiss franc, and the Japanese yen all against the U.S. dollar. All of a sudden, all four currencies shot in the opposite direction of their current movement, as if they had been shot out from cannon. I sat wondering what was going on. I was sure there were no scheduled fundamental announcements and, even if there were any announcements, an aggressive price movement after an announcement is approximately 240 pips in any specific direction and these markets had just moved approximately 500 pips! I was in shock. "Today is going to be a huge bloodbath for those traders who don't have any stops or protection, and one exceptional pay day for others," I thought, still not knowing what had caused such tremendous market movements.

All of a sudden, my phone rang, and my friend from Ada, Michigan, told me to turn on my TV.

He said, "A plane hit the World Trade Center."

I responded, "Unreal," and sat in disbelief, wondering how a pilot could not see those towers. Being a pilot myself, I thought maybe the pilot had fallen asleep or had a seizure. Just a few minutes later, a second plane hit the other tower.

The World Trade Center had special significance to my wife and I. While we were dating, I wanted so much to impress my wife and capture her heart that I would occasionally take her to New York. And just about every time we went, we visited the World Trade Center and ate at Windows on the World, the restaurant at the top of the first tower. Till this day, we hold those memories dear to our hearts.

All of a sudden, the news flashed, and the announcer reported that a plane had just struck the Pentagon and further stated, "It now appears America is under attack."

As we continued to watch this incredible, horrific event take place, I witnessed another amazing event unfold. As I turned to the markets and watched the currencies move, they moved in near perfect harmonic Fibonacci sequence, as if their movement was orchestrated by the finest market conductor in the world.

Figure 9-1 shows the movement on an hourly chart of the Swiss franc traded against the U.S. dollar. The Swiss franc fell 500 pips within four hours. After it bottomed out, it retraced immediately back to the exact Fibonacci 0.382, retracement level, bounced there, and then retraced further to past support, which was located at the Fibonacci 0.618 retracement level. There it bounced like a ball, hitting a concrete ceiling and then fell first to the 1.27 Fibonacci extension level, finding temporary support

FIGURE 9-1   CHF/USD (One-Hour Chart)

there before it moved to the designated 1.618 Fibonacci extension level, where it bottomed out, and settled down finding the final level of corresponding support in the down A, B, C, D move. Many other currencies responded in the same way.

Witnessing this tragic event and the market's methodical response was confirmation that the market is not this mysterious, chaotic place that most people fear. It is, in fact, a place where organized chaos and perfect balance exists, regardless of the situation. I witnessed the science of matter and energy interacting—the ebb and flow, the yin and yang, the action and reaction, all confirming that humans are the market.

Over the next few weeks, I couldn't help but think about what I had witnessed. Very little focus at that time was on the financial markets of the world. After all, America shut down the stock market for an entire week after September 11.

As the world searched for answers, the financial markets moved in near-perfect Fibonacci balance. Figure 9-2 is a chart of American Airlines stock, which was one of the airlines used in the attack. As you can see in the chart, the week before September 11, the market had already broken an

FIGURE 9-2   American Airlines (Hourly Chart)

uptrend line and entered into the sell zone. The stock then bounced off the backside of the uptrend line before it crowned and entered into its free fall. You can see the gap after September 11 when the stock market was closed. A week later, when it opened, the market free-fell to the 1.618 Fibonacci extension, forming a morning star confirming the bearish achievement of the 1.618 extension, and then proceeded to the 2.618 Fibonacci extension, but not before it stalled at the 1.618 extension.

Figure 9-3 is a chart of the Dow Jones Industrial. As you can see in the chart, in the two weeks before September 11, the market had already broken an uptrend line and entered into the sell zone. The Dow did not bounce off the backside of the uptrend line, rather, it kept dipping and waving as it fell, creating down A, B, C, D's. A week after, when the stock market opened, the Dow opened right at the 1.618 Fibonacci extension to the point, bounced up from there, then U-turned and proceeded onto the 2.618 Fibonacci extension, as if the stock market president or director instructed the 1.618 extension as a numerical opening.

If I really didn't know better, I would have to believe there was a conspiracy going on in the market.

FIGURE 9-3   Dow Jones (Hourly Chart)

Figure 9-4 is a chart of the S&P (Standard and Poors). As you can see, this chart somewhat emulates the Dow. After September 11, both markets (the S&P and the Dow) kept dipping and waving as it fell, creating down A, B, C, D's, and opened a week later in front of a 1.618/2.618 Fibonacci extension convergence from a previous down price swing, falling exactly to that convergence to the point, bouncing up from there, displaying an engulfing bullish candlestick formation, then U-turning and proceeding onto the 2.618 Fibonacci extension of the latter swing.

Watching the markets move during and after September 11 changed my life forever. The knowledge of the Fibonacci numerical sequence and how the numbers remained true to the sequence, even in times of tragedy, became one of my defining moments. I know that life can only be understood by looking backwards, but it must be lived by looking forward.

FIBONACCI RETRACEMENTS EVERYWHERE

I was in Vancouver, Canada, teaching a group of traders about the Fibonacci numbers in a conference room with a perfect view of the ocean

FIGURE 9-4   S & P 500 - Standard & Poor Indices (Hourly Chart)

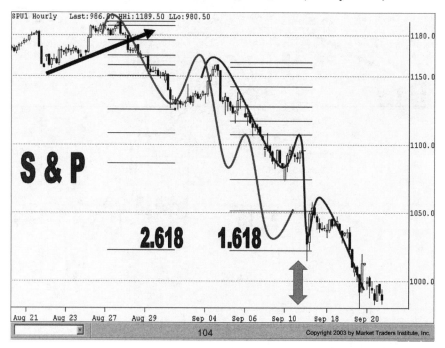

and the Rocky Mountains. As I went into greater detail about the Fibonacci retracement and extension numbers, I asked them to look at the mountains in the distance and envision a Fibonacci rally retracement and extension in the mountains, as seen in Figure 9-5. They sat in total disbelief as I pointed it out to them.

As if that was not enough proof, I asked them to look to the right and envision Mother Nature creating a downtrend, as she created the mountains accompanied with a downtrend line (see Figure 9-6).

Things in life don't change, we only change the way we look at them. Next time you are in the mountains, take the time to marvel at what Mother Nature created and how she did it in a numerical sequence. Or, the next time you are in an airplane, look down when you fly over a river and witness first-hand how gravity takes the river to the oceans or nearby lakes (see Figure 9-7).

Destiny is not a matter of chance, it is a matter of choice. If Columbus didn't discover that the world was round, somebody else would have. I guess part of my destiny is to point out to the world that the Fibonaccis can be found just about everywhere in nature, even in the market! Mother Nature obviously felt so strongly about the Fibonaccis that she wrote it in stone.

FIGURE 9-5   Fibonacci Sequence Seen in Mountains

Look at the Fibonacci Retracements and Extensions in Nature

If you ever have the opportunity to visit the Beverly Wilshire Hotel in Beverly Hills, California, please pay special attention to all the marble used in the bathrooms of their suites. The marble displays one of the greatest examples of the Fibonacci ratio numerical sequence written in stone as seen in Figure 9-8.

FIGURE 9-6   Fibonacci Sequence Seen in Valleys

Look at the Fibonacci Retracements and Extensions in Nature

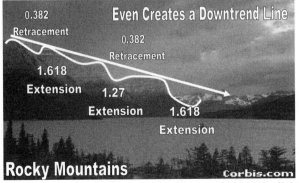

FIGURE 9-7   Fibonacci Sequence Seen in Rivers

Look at the Fibonacci Retracements and Extensions in Nature

0.786 Retracement

1.27 Extension

Qued Sebou River

Corbis.com

Copyright 2005 by Market Traders Institute, Inc.

FIGURE 9-8   Fibonacci Sequence Seen in Marble

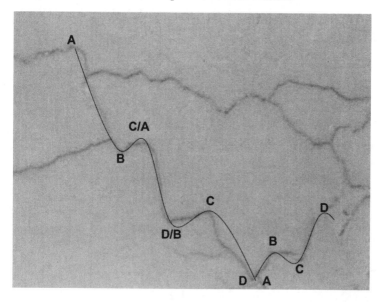

CONCLUSION

Life moves quickly, and it only takes one split-second to change it forever. September 11 proved that to most Americans.

I have come to learn that this world does not evolve around mankind, mankind evolves around nature. Mankind is not nature, it is only a part of nature living in this world, no different than all the other living creatures in the world. Unexpected things, even tragic events, happen to all living creatures. Most are totally beyond our control. It is not the tragic events that take place that change us forever, rather, it is what we do with our lives—the decisions we make after the tragic event takes place—that define who we are. Those critical decisions can build and create a beautiful life or they can destroy it.

10

FUNDAMENTAL ANALYSIS

FUNDAMENTAL ANNOUNCEMENTS ANALYSIS

Countries are managed, to a large degree, like companies. Some countries have a single leader they call a president, prime minister or king, much like the CEO (Chief Executive Officer), President or Managing Director of a Company. Other countries have a ruling body called a house of commons, a senate or a congress, much like a corporation's board of directors. Countries produce goods or services for consumption and so do companies (see Figure 10-1).

Companies issue stock certificates enabling individuals outside the original founders to participate in its growth and financial benefits, just as countries do with their currency. The currency you carry around or place in a savings account is your stock certificate or part ownership of that country.

If a company grows, as a rule, the stock certificate increases in value. If the company incurs too much debt, has a bad year or two, or ends up with bad leadership, the share value decreases. A country is the same. If the country grows economically in comparison with other countries around the world, the value of its currency will grow in proportion to the devaluation of another country's currency.

If you have acquired a sufficient amount of currency from a particular country, whether it be by inheritance or by hard work, you may choose

FIGURE 10-1   Country Versus Company

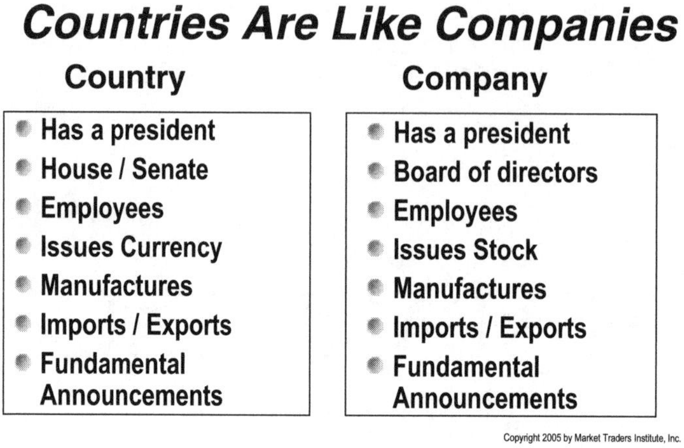

Countries Are Like Companies

Country	Company

● Has a president
● House / Senate
● Employees
● Issues Currency
● Manufactures
● Imports / Exports
● Fundamental
   Announcements
	● Has a president
	● Board of directors
	● Employees
	● Issues Stock
	● Manufactures
	● Imports / Exports
	● Fundamental
	   Announcements

to keep it in that country. If you are educated about the world economy, you may prefer the economic stability of another country versus the one you live in and choose to save your money elsewhere. For example, let's say you live in Venezuela and do not feel safe with the way the leader is running the country but you feel fairly secure about America. You may earn your money in Venezuela but save it in America by converting your bolivars into U.S. dollars.

What happens to the value of a stock when earnings did not meet expectations, or an officer is caught stealing from the company, or the president sells 80 percent of his shares or holdings in the company? The value of the company share goes down. Investors start to believe that management is not keeping its eye on the ball, they become insecure about the company as a whole, and they begin to sell their stock. When more people sell shares of a company versus buying shares, the value of the share goes down. Conversely, what happens if a company announces that it has created a revolutionary product and will need to increase its employees by 20 percent? Investors may get excited and start a buying frenzy of the company stocks and drive the share value up. The news that comes out about a company, good or bad, is called a *fundamental announcement.*

Countries and companies both have fundamental announcements, which have similar effects on the value of a country's currency as it will have on a company's share price. The same effect that unemployment at an all-time high or housing starts at an all-time low have on currency values is similar to what happens if the prime minister resigns or if the married president is caught cheating on his wife with an intern. Bad news like this drives down the value of the currency. People get nervous and feel the leadership is in disarray and may move their money out of the country and into another country in hopes of preserving the value of their estate.

When investors get nervous, for whatever reason, and want to move their money from one country to another, it is called *fleeing to safety*. They move their money from one country to another, creating a buying frenzy around the currency they are acquiring, driving the value up, and creating a selling frenzy around the currency they are selling, which drives the value of that currency down. If the masses start selling more than buying—stock or currency—it will drive prices down. Selling U.S. dollars and converting them to Japanese yen will drive the value of the U.S. dollar down and the Japanese yen up.

America declares war on Iraq. Investors know a war will create hardship for the country, its leadership, and its people. Employment may go down due to a weakened economy during wartime. If the country gets into trouble fighting the war and needs to borrow money to continue, other countries may be hesitant to lend it money because the enemy might win, take over the country, and make it more difficult for the borrower to pay the loan back. That being the case, the country becomes a high-risk borrower and must pay a higher interest rate, which increases its debt, to acquire the funds it needs.

If leadership, the economy, and the war start to get out of hand, investors may get nervous about leaving their money in, for example, America and want to move it to perhaps a country like Great Britain. If a lot of investors feel that way, they will flee to safety and start selling their U.S. dollars and buying British pounds. As a result, this will drive the U.S. dollar down in value and the British pound up.

Just as every public corporation has a set of announcements that inform investors about the overall health and well-being of the company, so do countries have similar announcements. In both cases, the announcements allow investors to either buy more stock or currency, sell what they have, or stay neutral. These announcements are fundamental announcements.

In the currency market or on the Forex, each country around the world has approximately 20 major fundamental announcements annually for investors to monitor. The importance of the announcements shifts as the economy shifts. Governments report the health and overall economic well-being of a country to investors via fundamental announcements, which are the economic indicators of the country.

Even though most economic reports are created monthly, quarterly, and yearly, some are created weekly. Some economic indicators or reports carry more weight than others. Some examples of such economic reports are the Gross Domestic Product (GDP), Employment and Non-farm Payroll. Investors should watch the monthly, quarterly, and yearly economic reports, but the weekly versions of the same report are of less importance. All economic reports are posted on a governmental calendar, giving the date, time, and the forecast or expectation of change, as well as the previous percentage change (see Figure 10-2).

You can keep up with all major government reports that affect the Forex at www.markettraders.com or www.forextips.com, under the heading "Economic Reports", or in leading newspapers, such as the *Wall Street Journal*, the *Financial Times*, or the *New York Times*. Although newspapers are great resources for information on fundamental announcements, the Internet is now the number one source for investors.

FIGURE 10-2   Fundamental Announcements

Time (New York Time)	Location	Description	Forecast	Previously
12/23 10:00	US	Nov New Home Sales	1.2 mln	1.226 mln
12/23 09:45	US	Dec Univ. of Michigan Sent. Survey – final	95.7	95.7
12/23 08:30	US	Nov Personal Spending	0.2%	0.7%
12/23 08:30	US	Nov Core PCE Price Index	1.4%	1.5%
12/23 08:30	US	Nov Personal Income	0.3%	0.6%
12/23 08:30	CAN	Oct Real GDP	0.2%	0.0%
12/23 08:30	US	Weekly Jobless Claims	335K	317K
12/23 08:30	US	Nov Durable Goods Orders	0.5%	-0.4%
12/23 08:30	US	Nov Durable Goods Orders ex transport.	0.8%	-0.7%

When a fundamental announcement is about to occur, investors usually stop buying or selling right before the announcement. If the news is good, prices may go up, and if it is bad, prices may go down. Either way, to play it safe, they usually wait until the announcement is read before they take a position in the market. Within seconds after the announcement is read, a frenzy of buying or selling starts to take place, potentially creating a dramatic price change in only a couple of seconds.

Let us say you are trading and waiting for Mr. Ben Bernanke, chairman of the Federal Reserve Bank of the United States, to announce a potential U.S. interest rate change at 2:30 p.m. EST, approximately 10 hours from now. The current interest rate is at 4.5 percent. There are three possible scenarios that could result from the announcement: the interest rate could go up, it could go down, or it could remain unchanged. Let us look at possible cause and effect scenarios:

Cause: Interest rates go up, and as a result the cost to borrow money increases. When the cost of borrowing money goes up, fewer people will be interested in borrowing money.

Effect: The demand for U.S. dollars will go down, and fewer people will buy the U.S. dollar, creating a weaker dollar.

Cause: Interest rates go down, meaning the cost to borrow money will decline. When the cost of borrowing money goes down, more people will be interested in borrowing money.

Effect: The demand for U.S. dollars rises, and more people buy the U.S. dollar, creating a stronger dollar.

Cause: Interest rates go unchanged.

Effect: The value of the U.S. dollar should not change and remains the same.

If interest rates increase or decrease, currency values increase or decrease. If you watch the economic indicators of the world and try to trade making money off the rate of change, you are considered a fundamentalist trader. If you trade or take positions based on reading a chart, which I have been teaching you, you are called a technical trader. (Technical analysis is the study of chart reading.) To be a good trader, you need to create a balance between the technicals and the fundamentals. However, the most successful traders of the world are predominately technical traders rather than fundamentals traders.

I will never forget back in the early 2000s, a neighbor of mine gave me a call one morning to say, "Jared, I really need your help."

I said, "I will try my best. What is your situation?"

He said, "I own about $300,000 in Microsoft stock. It had a value at one time of about $500,000 and is down to about $300,000, and I don't want it to fall any further."

I said, "I don't blame you! Now let me ask you this, are you calling because you think I can increase its value for you? I am the FXCHIEF, not the STOCKCHIEF, you know," I told him, laughing.

Then, with a serious voice, he said, "As you know, the U.S. government sued Microsoft for violating monopoly laws and the judge is going to rule Monday morning on the issue." He continued, "Can I get you to look at a Microsoft chart ASAP and help me out here?"

I asked, "What do you want to know?

He said, "Can you tell me whether I should sell all my stock today or hold onto to it?"

I said, "Are you kidding me? This is a no-win situation. If I advise you incorrectly, you will burn my house down. And if I'm correct, you will ignore me as you drive by my house on your way to dinner in your new Mercedes."

We both laughed again, and I said, "Give me a minute and I will pull up a chart on Microsoft." Now, as I was pulling up the chart, I was thinking to myself, here is a person investing $300,000 to $500,000 in one stock, who knows what all his holdings are, yet he won't even take the time to educate to himself on how the markets work technically. After all, he openly admitted he was down $200,000 from $500,000. I thought, a simple little lesson on trend lines, trend line breaks, and buy and sell zones could have saved him $200,000.

After looking at the chart, I said, "Here is what I think. The judge is going to rule in favor of Microsoft on Monday morning."

He said, "You're kidding, right?"

I said, "Maybe yes, maybe no."

He said, "Come on! Get serious here and help me out. You know what you are doing and I don't."

I said, "Look here, Ken, this is my analysis. The reason I said the judge is going to rule in favor of Microsoft is, technically, the Microsoft chart has been in a downtrend, it has broken the downtrend line, entered into the buy zone, returned to resistance, and is now forming up A, B, C, D's and is at an 0.618 Fibonacci retracement level/up C and a beautiful morning star has just formed."

He said, "All-righty then," with a hint of sarcasm. "Look Jared, that is all Greek to me. But what I think you are saying is that you want me to hold my position?"

I said, "No, that is not what I am saying."

"So you want me to dump everything today?" He asked in a voice of frustration.

I quickly responded, "No, that is not what I said either."

He then yelled at me, screaming, "What should I do, I can't afford to lose any more money!"

Eventually, I calmly said, "The reason I am so adamant that the judge will rule in favor of Microsoft is that I believe, in situations like this, nature knows ahead of time what needs to happen to keep everything in balance. The charts predominately tell the trader ahead of time what is going to happen next in the market."

He interrupted me, saying, "Really?" as if I was smoking dope.

I went on, "Be that as it may, tornadoes can come out of nowhere."

I went on, saying, "Here is what I would do. As I said, it is my analysis that Microsoft is going to rally after the judge announces his verdict. So I would stay in my position today, but tell your broker you want to put in a stop order at around $2.00 a share lower than where it is trading today. I would then dump half of the shares there and keep the other half as a long-term investment, as we both know Microsoft is not going out of business anytime soon."

Well, to his surprise, but not mine, the charts were right. The judge ruled in favor of Microsoft and the stock rallied like a rocket. He went to dinner in his new Mercedes while I stayed home. I haven't heard from him since.

TRADING DAYS VERSUS TRENDING DAYS

Trading days are when there are no fundamental announcements. Currency charts move typically 60 to 90 pips, and sometimes 120 pips, depending on the currency. Trending days are fundamental announcement days, when the market will generally take off in a direction after the announcement and move 120 to 240 pips within the first five hours, incurring a major price change. It then often stays at that new price for the remainder of the day.

Novice traders prefer trading days as the market is typically more predictable. Expert traders, however, prefer trending days over trading days because you can make more money in less time.

If there is a major change, or a major projected change, anticipated in the economy, with the impact of an economic fundamental announcement, the prices will move (see Figure 10-3).

FIGURE 10-3   EUR/USD (One-Hour Chart)

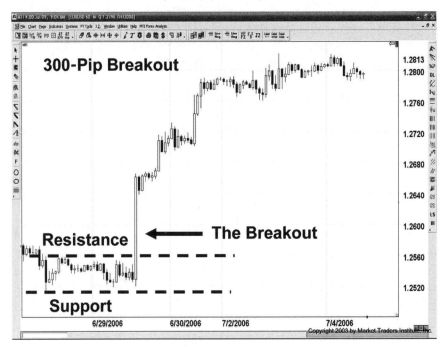

Before the announcement, traders stop trading, and the chart begins to consolidate. Consolidation, or *bracketing*, in a chart is a potential sign that a fundamental announcement is about to take place; traders are waiting for the announcement before taking any new positions. Trading appears to be thin, or what is also referred to as *light*. After the announcement, if there is a percentage change from the previous report, there will be a breakout from that consolidation, as you see in Figure 10-3. After the announcement, traders aggressively start buying or selling, which creates a breakout. In this particular chart, a buying frenzy ensued and prices broke out to the north.

In the event of no change after the announcement, the chart will usually continue in the direction of the previous trend.

INCREASED RISK WITH TRADING FUNDAMENTAL ANNOUNCEMENTS

Traders must be very careful if they want to trade during fundamental announcements. Years back, Forex brokers allowed traders to straddle the consolidation, which means you place a buy above the consolidation and a sell below the consolidation, right before the announcement. When the market broke out, it would automatically take you with it, in the direction of the breakout. Brokers ended up losing a lot of money to traders through this process, due to their inability to offset the trades fast enough in the interbank market. They have now pretty much eliminated the practice of straddling.

Today, if you want to trade a fundamental announcement, you either need to be in the market before the announcement or try to get a fill right after the announcement. When trying to get a fill right after the announcement, you risk the danger of being slipped perhaps 30 to 100 pips, as the market rapidly moves in a direction. There have been times, and will continue to be times, when the market moves 200 pips inside of 20 seconds after an announcement. Fundamental announcements can be very volatile and create *whiplashes*, as seen in Figures 10-4 and 10-5, resulting in heavy losses.

FIGURE 10-4   EUR/USD (One-Hour Chart)

FIGURE 10-5   GBP/USD (One-Hour Chart)

WORLD ECONOMIES

There are three major world economies and time zones that traders monitor:

1.   The Asian market
2.   The European market (which consists mainly of Great Britain)
3.   The U.S. market

The majority of Forex trading transactions are done in Great Britain. More than 75 percent of all Forex transactions are done during the trading session of the European market. The majority of the $1.5 trillion U.S. dollars of transactions daily are done within the seven major world currencies.

Small retail traders trade the six major world currencies—EUR, GBP, CHF, JPY, CAD, and AUD against the U.S. dollar—however, most are paid in U.S. dollars.

The sun doesn't set on the financial markets of the world. As a matter of fact, the sun never sets—the world continually turns. As the world turns, the financial markets of the world open and close. Somewhere in this world, a financial market is open during any given 24-hour period.

At 7 p.m. EST, the Asian markets open (8 a.m. local Asian time) and
continue for approximately 8 hours.
At 3 a.m. EST, the European markets open (8 a.m. local British time)
and continue for approximately 8 hours.
At 8 a.m. EST, the American markets open and continue for 8 hours.

You can see that the three markets overlap each other, although the
majority of volume is traded during the European and U.S. sessions. That is
where you will find the majority of price movement during any given
24-hour period.

If you have an interest in trading what are called *off-currencies,* or
currencies other than the majors, you may want to monitor the particular
country's economic calendar. For example, if you want to trade the Australian dollar against the New Zealand dollar, you may want to do some
research on the major announcements that could affect those two currencies. Keep in mind that the importance of the announcements may change
from time to time. If the economy of the country is really suffering, retail
sales will play an important roll and may be an indicator of potential major
change. That specific announcement may create a very volatile currency
market during their struggling economic times. However, if the economy is
good, retail sales may not have much of an effect at all on price change,
regardless of the percentage change in the report.

THE IMPORTANCE OF FUNDAMENTAL ANNOUNCEMENTS

Fundamental announcements have an effect on every country's currency in
some way, either immediately or soon after. The reserve bank of every country monitors the inflation of the country by using economic indicators.
When these reflect inflationary pressure, the bank will generally increase
interest rates. When signs of deflation are present, interest rates are
generally lowered. Interest rates are important for the economy because they
influence the willingness of individuals and households to borrow money
and make investments. An increase in interest rates will cause a downturn in
the economy, whereas a decrease will stimulate the economic growth.

THE 13 MOST IMPORTANT U.S. FUNDAMENTAL ANNOUNCEMENTS

The following are fundamentals announced in the United States:

Purchasing Managers Index (Chicago PMI): This announcement is
based on surveys of more than 200 purchasing managers in the manufacturing industry who are based in the Chicago area. This distribution of

manufacturing firms mirrors the national distribution in the United States. Readings above 50 percent indicate an expanding factory sector, whereas values below 50 percent are indicative of contraction. This announcement is made on the last business day of every month at 10 a.m. EST.

Consumer Confidence Index (CCI): This is a survey of 5,000 consumers monitoring their attitudes toward the current situation and expectations regarding economic conditions. This report can occasionally be helpful in predicting sudden shifts in the economy. It can also give a trader an idea about the direction of the U.S. economy. Only index changes of at least five points should be considered significant. The announcement is made on the last Tuesday of every month at 10 a.m. EST.

Consumer Price Index (CPI): CPI measures the change in price of a representative basket of goods and services, such as food, energy, housing, clothing, transportation, medical care, entertainment, and education. It is also known as the *cost-of-living index*. It is important because it excludes food and energy prices for it's monthly stability, referred to as the *core CPI*, and gives a clearer picture of the underlying inflation trend. This announcement is made around the 13th of every month at 8:30 a.m. EST.

Durable Goods Orders: The official name of this announcement is the "Advance Report on Durable Goods Manufacturers, Shipments and Orders." It is a government index that reflects the dollar volume of orders, shipments, and unfilled orders of durable goods. Durable goods are new or used items with a normal life expectancy of three years or more. This generally excludes defense and transportation orders because of their volatility. This report gives the trader information on the strength of demand for U.S. manufactured durable goods—from both domestic and foreign sources. An increase in the index suggests that demand is strengthening, which may result in rising production and employment. A falling index obviously indicates the opposite. The data is released around the 26th of every month at 8:30 a.m. EST.

Employment Situation: This report lists the number of payroll jobs at all non-farm business establishments and government agencies. The unemployment rate, average hourly and weekly earnings, and the length of the average workweek are all listed in this report. This release is the single most closely watched economic statistic because of its timelines, accuracy, and its importance as an indicator of economic activity. It plays a big role in influencing financial market psychology during the month.

Non-farm Payroll Indicator: This fundamental is a co-incident indicator of economic growth. The greater the increase in employment figures, the faster the total economy will grow. An increasing unemployment rate is associated with a contracting economy and declining interest rates. A decreasing unemployment rate is associated with an expanding economy and potentially increasing interest rates. The fear is that wages will rise if the unemployment rate becomes too low and workers are hard to find. The economy is considered to be at full employment when unemployment is between 5.5 and 6 percent. The data is released on the first Friday of every month at 8:30 a.m. EST.

Existing Home Sales: This report measures the selling rate of preowned houses and is considered a decent indicator of activity in the housing sector. It provides a gauge of not only the demand for housing but also the economic momentum. People have to be financially confident in order to buy a house. The data is announced on the 25th of every month at 10 a.m. EST.

Gross Domestic Product (GDP): GDP measures the dollar value of goods and services produced within the borders of the United States, regardless of who owns the assets or the nationality of the labor used in producing that output. This is the most comprehensive measure of the performance of the U.S. economy. Healthy GDP growth is between 2.0 and 2.5 percent (when the unemployment rate is between 5.5 and 6 percent). A higher GDP growth leads to accelerating inflation, and lower growth indicates a weak economy. This data is released in the third or fourth week of every month at 8:30 a.m. EST.

New Home Sales: This report is based on interviews with approximately 10,000 builders, or owners of about 15,000 selected building projects. It measures the number of newly constructed homes with a committed sale during the month. It is considered an indication of near-term spending for housing-related items and of consumer spending in general. However, investors prefer the existing home sales report, which accounts for around 84 percent of all houses sold earlier in the month.

Philadelphia Fed: This is a regional manufacturing index that covers Pennsylvania, New Jersey, and Delaware, which represents a reasonable cross section of national manufacturing activities. Readings above 50 percent indicate an expanding factory sector, whereas values below 50 percent indicate contraction. The data is released on the third Thursday of every month at 10 a.m. EST.

Producer Price Index (PPI): The PPI measures the average price of a fixed basket of capital and consumer goods at the wholesale level, which gives a clearer indication of the underlying inflation trend. There are three primary publication structures for the PPI: industry, commodity, and stage-of-processing. It's important to monitor the PPI excluding food and energy prices for its monthly stability. This announcement is made around the 11th of every month at 8:30 a.m. EST.

Retail Sales: This index measures the total sales of goods by all retail establishments in the United States (sales of services are not included). These figures are in current dollars, which means they are not adjusted for inflation; however, the data is adjusted for seasonal, holiday, and trading-day differences between months of the year. The retail sales index is considered the timeliest indicator of broad consumer spending patterns, providing a sense of the trends among different types of retailers. These trends can help you spot specific investment opportunities. The data is released around the 12th of every month at 8:30 a.m. EST.

International Trade: This report measures the difference between exports and imports of U.S. goods and services. Imports and exports are important components of aggregate economic activity—representing approximately 14 percent and 12 percent of the GDP, respectively. Typically, stronger exports are bullish for the dollar. The data is announced on the 19th of every month at 8:30 a.m. EST.

The above economic indicators are the most relevant for the six major world currencies on the Forex market, but that does not mean they are the only ones. Once again, you can keep up with all major government reports that affect the Forex at www.markettraders.com or www.forextips.com, under the heading "Economic Reports". I strongly suggest you review the economic calendar daily before you trade in order to be prepared for any surprise movements in the market.

CONCLUSION

Tracking down the fundamental announcements before you trade is critical. Make it a habit to see if there are any major fundamental announcements about to take place, which may create volatility.

Trading during fundamental announcements can be like riding the rapids in a river, whereas trading during non–fundamental days can be like riding in the calm part of the river. I recommend that the novice trader shy away from trading during potentially volatile times, staying focused on only trading what you understand. Do not ever trade with a sense of false security, thinking that the environment is going to be calm because you checked with the economic calendar and there were no announcements. All it takes is an attempted assassination of a president, an unscheduled announcement of an interest rate change, or a September 11 type event, and that calm trading environment will suddenly turn hostile and volatile. Whenever an unexpected announcement or event takes place, it can have a major impact on prices in the market.

11

CONSOLIDATING, BRACKETING, ACCUMULATION, OR SIDEWAYS MOVEMENT

L IFE IN GENERAL needs to be kept simple—people have a tendency to complicate it—and trading consolidation needs to be kept simple as well. The market can only move up, down, or sideways. If the market is not trending up or down, it is moving in sideways, which is commonly referred to as *consolidation* (see Figure 11-1).

In Chapter 10, I pointed out the relevance of fundamental announcements, and we looked at their importance, as well as the effect they have on the market and the price of the different currencies. Although the market consolidates in a tight trading range right before a fundamental announcement, this is not the only consolidation that exists.

Believe it or not, the market consolidates 50 to 60 percent of the time and trends the remainder of the time. That is why traders who create

FIGURE 11-1   GBP/USD (One-Hour Chart)

trading systems for trending markets lose all their money when the market
starts to go sideways. If you are going to use a trading system, you really
need to trade two different trading systems: one that spots trends and allows
you to take advantage of them, and one that spots consolidations and allows
you to take advantage of them.

Learning how to spot and trade in sideways markets is every bit as profitable to a trader as is trading a trend. When the market consolidates, it
creates equal levels of support and resistance within a trading range.
Trading ranges vary in size per chart and from one time frame to the next.
They can range as little as 30 pips on an hour chart to as much as 400 pips
on a daily chart, and even larger (see Figure 11-2).

CONSOLIDATION FACTORS

There are two primary reasons why a market starts to consolidate, accumu-
late, bracket, or go sideways.

FIGURE 11-2   GBP/USD (One-Hour Chart)

The first reason for a consolidation is when the world is waiting for a fundamental announcement and traders stop trading in anticipation of a major market move or breakout after the announcement. When traders stop trading, the market begins to consolidate in what is called *a tight trading range*, or a *small trading range*. Small trading ranges are found on smaller time frames and are between 20 to 60 pips. They can be seen on smaller time frames such as the 60-minute and 30-minute charts (see Figure 11-3).

The second reason the market may consolidate could be due to a country intervening and wanting its currency to trade within a certain trading range for economic reasons. Many times countries will want their currency to stay within a trading range of, say four cents. For example, if Japan wanted their currency to stabilize between 108 and 112 yen to the U.S. dollar, that is a 400-pip range. The reason they may want the market to stay there could be for importing and exporting reasons, or perhaps they found this to be a good price that spurs imports or exports. If that is the case, the markets may go sideways for extended periods of time.

Large trading ranges are between 150 and 400 pips or even larger. They can extend over a longer period of time, such as a few weeks or even a few

FIGURE 11-3   EUR/USD (One-Hour Chart)

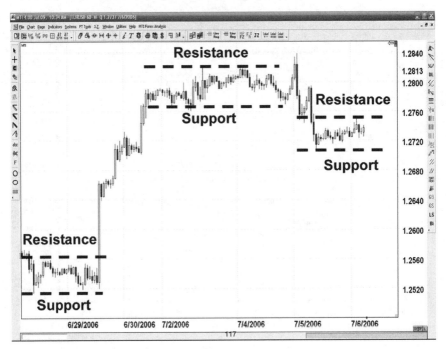

months. They are easily seen on larger time frames, such as four- to eight-hour charts, or daily charts. In Figure 11-4, the euro consolidated inside a three-cent trading range for well over a month.

With the market only able to go up, down, or sideways, and having the market locked in a sideways range 50 to 60 percent of the time, learning how to trade the two types of consolidations in the market can be financially advantageous.

There are three trading strategies to use when the markets are consolidating, accumulating, or bracketing.

STRATEGY 1

This strategy is suitable for large trading ranges between 150 and 300 pips. As the market rallies toward resistance, the bulls will incur a tremendous amount of resistance at or near the highs. What is actually taking place in the market is that major banks and financial institutions are entering the market and beginning to sell aggressively, creating more sellers than buyers. Consequently, prices fall.

FIGURE 11-4   EUR/USD (Four-Hour Chart)

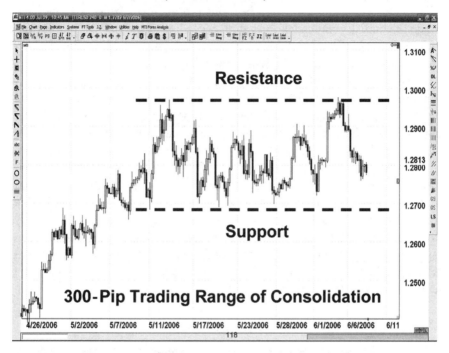

During periods of consolidation, traders will look to sell at resistance or near the highs. What successful traders do is look into their trader's toolbox to see what else they can use to confirm their decision to sell. When prices get close to resistance, most traders turn to smaller time frames and look for confirming bearish Japanese candlestick formations near the highs, and then short the market after the bearish formation appears, according to the rules of that specific candlestick formation. The bearish candlestick formation gives confirmation that the market is about to U-turn. They then turn back to a larger time frame and look to find support on the other side of the consolidation trading range, taking the ride back down to support.

As prices begin to fall and get closer to the level of support, once again major banks and financial institutions will enter the market, and there will be a change of the tide from bearish to bullish, due to more buyers than sellers. If the consolidation is going to hold, prices will then U-turn and begin to rally. When prices get close to another level of support, once again, traders will look to confirm their decision to buy and look for bullish

Japanese candlestick formations near a level of support or a prominent low. They will enter going long after the bullish formation appears, and they will trade the bullish candlestick formation according to the rules of that formation and within the guidelines of equity management (which will be discussed in Chapter 12). The bullish candlestick formation gives confirmation that the market is about to U-turn. A trader then needs to turn back to a larger time frame and look at where resistance is currently and take the ride back up to the level of resistance. Traders can repeat this process over and over again for weeks or months, until the market breaks out of the range.

If you think about it, once you find consolidation, it is hard to get hurt. As long as you have the patience to wait for the bearish candlestick formation to appear near the level of resistance and a bullish candlestick formation to appear near a level of support. The beauty of waiting for candlestick formations to appear in the consolidation is that when the market is ready to break out of consolidation, a candlestick formation will usually *not* appear (see Figure 11-5). This would make trading too simple. You need to sell at the level of resistance and buy at a level of support when you find a consolidation in the market.

FIGURE 11-5   EUR/USD (Four-Hour Chart)

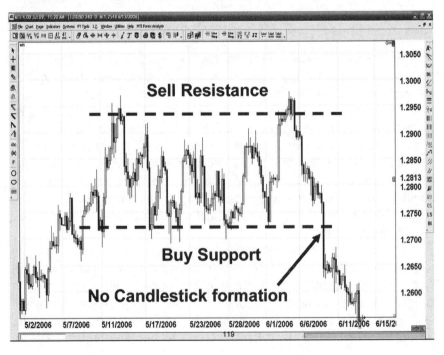

STRATEGY 2

This strategy will work provided your broker will allow you to trade this way (currently at www. I-TradeFX. com, a Forex Broker, you can straddle the market in this fashion). Please check with your broker first before attempting to trade using this strategy. Because of the increased volume of people wanting to trade the fundamentals, not all brokers can handle the increased trading volume during announcements.

This strategy is called a *straddle* and was designed for trading in tight trading ranges in anticipation of a fundamental announcement. It is very important that there is a fundamental announcement to be released and that the market range is between 20 and 60 pips. In order to trade a straddle effectively, the market needs to create a tight level of consolidation before the announcement, which, in turn, will provide a straddle opportunity. As a rule, the longer the market has been in the range, the more aggressive the outbreak will be (see Figure 11-6).

When you see consolidation forming before a fundamental announcement, turn to a smaller time frame, such as a 30-minute chart. Place your straddle orders five minutes before the announcement is made. Place a buy

FIGURE 11-6   EUR/USD (One-Hour Chart)

order 15 pips above or north of the resistance level and 10 pips below or south of the level of support, or the trading range. Why 15 pips above and 10 pips below? All currencies have a bid-ask spread that is between 3 and 5 pips. Place your stop-loss orders 15 pips above the last high for the sell order and 10 pips below the last low for the buy order. The reason your buy entry order is 15 pips above the last high is because traders look at bid charts, which reflect the selling price at a particular moment. Because there is a spread between the bid and the ask price, we need to add the extra 5 pips to compensate for the difference. This precaution will keep you from being taken into the market too early.

You should also consider not trading if the trading range of the consolidation is greater than the amount of money you are willing to lose should the trade not work out. Always remember that the market can break out in either direction.

It is important that you create two trading plans with entry points, stop-loss orders, and limit orders for profit in both directions. It is also important to mentally work through a "what if" scenario. You need to remember the market can go north or south. If the market goes south, look for past levels of support to exit with a profit before the bears score any points and begin pulling back. The opposite will take place if the buy order is triggered first—look for past levels of resistance to exit with a profit before the bulls score any points by taking out those highs or past levels of resistance. Bulls also pull back after making a new high and scoring a point.

NOT ALL FUNDAMENTAL ANNOUNCEMENTS MOVE THE MARKET

In theory, the market should not move if the numbers from the economic or fundamental report do not differ from the previous announcement. But trading is not an exact science. The market can move whichever way it wants, whenever it wants. If the market breaks out of consolidation and triggers one of your entry orders and then returns into consolidation, perhaps there was mixed sentiment in the market and everyone is changing direction. If the market breaks out of consolidation and returns back to consolidation, technically the market will then go the other way, which is why you may want to keep the second order in place, allowing you to take advantage of the market reversal.

During any fundamental announcement, the market is very volatile—anything is possible. If the market reverses, the only way to recoup your losses after you have been stopped out by the first order is to have the courage to leave the other order in and change direction. You must be agile as you trade and you must be quick to change from being a bull to becoming a bear. Charts talk, and you need to listen to what the market is telling you.

To be a good trader, you must trade by the chart and not by your heart. You must listen to the market with your eyes and respond accordingly with no feeling or emotion attached to any given trade.

STRATEGY 3

Should you spot consolidation, rule number one is to check to see if there is a fundamental announcement in the near future. Many times a consolidation will appear because the market is open 24 hours a day, and during later afternoon trading is light. In this case, the simplest strategy is it to continue to trade in the direction of the previous trend.

Should you spot consolidation without a fundamental announcement in sight, do not be like Roger, one of our students who shared this experience.

Roger returned to class and started off telling us about some of the great results he experienced trading straddles and consolidations in the market. He told us about how he got all excited and told his wife to get ready for dinner because they were going out on the town to celebrate. He entered a trade during a straddle in the market and, just like clockwork, the market took him in. He yelled at his wife, "Come on honey, pour me some champagne, I see nothing but good times filled with wealth and prosperity taking place tonight."

All of a sudden the market U-turned, went back into consolidation, and started to go the other way. "I was so excited when I saw that consolidation, all I could think about was the money I had made trading a straddle breakout, and I forgot to do the two most important things—see if there were any fundamental announcements and, two, put in a protective stop-loss order on my trade," he said.

"After about an hour, the market had moved about 60 pips against me and I was trading two lots at the time. I realized I was $1,200 down. At that moment, my wife came downstairs all dressed up, ready to go to dinner, champagne bottle in hand." He said he looked at his wife, grabbed the bottle of champagne out of her hand, took a big swig and said, "Where do you think you are going?" Everyone in the class burst out laughing. I guess we have to experience pain every now and then as a reminder to pay attention to the details.

I have learned it is better to be out of a trade wishing you were in than to be in a trade wishing you were out!

If you see a consolidation forming, always check for fundamental announcements first to determine if you should trade in that market. If there are no fundamental announcements, then go ahead and trade in the direction of the current trend. If you forget to check the above two important rules, you will probably be introduced to what is called a *bull trap* or a *bear trap*.

BULL AND BEAR TRAPS

If you spot consolidation and you straddle the market without checking the economic calendar for fundamental announcements, you will likely get caught in a trap.

BULL TRAPS

After consolidation has formed and there are no fundamental announcements, bull traps are false breakouts to the south out of that consolidation, doing nothing more than fulfilling the natural numerical sequence of the market, then U-turning back in the direction of the previous trend, moving

FIGURE 11-7   EUR/USD (30-Minute Chart)

FIGURE 11-8   USD/CAD (One-Hour Chart)

towards the Fibonacci D extension level. In other words, the market begins to consolidate inside the natural A, B, C, D formation of a price swing. There are no scheduled fundamental announcements, and the market is simply following the Fibonacci numerical sequence as it slowly moves in the direction of the previous trend (see Figure 11-7).

BEAR TRAPS
Bear traps are the opposite of bull traps. After consolidation has formed and there are no fundamental announcements, bear traps are false breakouts to the north that do nothing more than hit a Fibonacci retracement level and then U-turn back in the direction of the previous trend, moving towards the Fibonacci D extension (see Figure 11-8).

CONCLUSION
Most fundamental announcements create a dramatic change in the market. Remember, the only thing in life that remains consistent is change. Currencies may aggressively react to fundamental announcements or they may

not. Successful and educated traders respond, rather than react, to those announcements. They are well prepared and ready to switch from being a bull to becoming a bear at the drop of a hat. Trading on the Forex with or without fundamental announcements can create an environment where there are unexpected surprises, creating trading ranges of perhaps 150 to 300 pips in a single four- to five-hour trading session.

Your future depends on many things when you trade. In this market, it depends mostly on you—your education, your emotions, and what you do with them. Trading consolidations can be very exciting and profitable if you know how to trade them correctly.

Hopefully, this chapter will place you in position to take advantage of the markets during consolidation so the market does not take advantage of you.

12

LEARNING THE RULES OF EQUITY MANAGEMENT

WHAT IS EQUITY MANAGEMENT?

I wanted to place this chapter at the beginning of the book, but the more I thought about it, the more I felt it really needed to be at the end. It's about financial losses. No matter where I go, I seem to hear story after story about traders who lost money in the market.

As I have listened to each trader's personal experience, I have always been tempted to ask two simple questions:

1.   Was the loss of money worth all the emotional pain and financial heartache?
2.   If you had the opportunity to do that trade or investment again, what would you do differently?

So tell me your tale of loss:

1.   What is the biggest loss you have personally taken in the market?
2.   If you have never traded in the market, what is the biggest loss you have taken as an investor or in business?

3.   What was your emotional experience during this event?

4.   What went through your head and your heart during that event?

5.   Were you in emotional control or was your destructive ego in control?

6.   Was it worth it?

7.   What did you learn from this experience? If nothing, then I am sad to inform you that you will probably repeat it in the future.

8.   What new disciplines have you now implemented when you invest or trade to protect yourself against losses?

Trading in the markets is a fantasy or dream to most people. For some reason, they think something magical is going to take place and *poof*, they will become rich. They don't try to understand it because they believe there is nothing to be understood. They believe it is mysterious and accept that it just works that way. Well, it *can* be understood.

The market is not a mysterious or magical place. It can be figured out, and people can make money over and over as they come to this trading wishing well.

If you have experienced trading on the Forex, and you tried to outsmart the market by not protecting yourself by trading with a stop-loss order, let me ask you this; how many pips did the market move against you? 100? 200? 300 pips? Did it come back to your entry or were you liquidated? If it did come back in your financial favor, did you continue to stay in to capture 100, 200, or 300 pips in profit, keeping your risk-reward ratios intact? Or were you so traumatized and emotionally beat up that when it came back, you were just too grateful and happy to get out at breakeven or with only 3 to 5 pips of profit, in fear that the market would take it all away again? I know the feeling, I have been there, too.

I remember sitting on our back porch one evening with my wife, after one of my many emotional rollercoaster rides in the market; I looked at my wife and said, "You know, if the government called me up for active duty and asked me to go to war, I wouldn't have one scared bone in my body. I think learning to trade on the Forex is much worse than fighting any war." Traders who have attempted to day trade with limited knowledge can certainly appreciate what I am saying.

After I finally learned how to trade, I realized how important it was to protect myself at all times. As you learn to trade (or do anything new in your life) never forget rule no. 1: *Protect yourself at all times.*

When you drive, when you are at work, when you are on vacation, when you are swimming in oceans, rivers, and lakes, always remember to protect yourself. Always protect yourself when you enter into a loving relationship, when you lend money to your friends and family, when you make a new investment. Always protect yourself—this is vital to your financial survival!

Protecting yourself as you trade is called placing a protective stop-loss order in the market at the same time as you execute the trade. Protecting yourself as you trade is quantifying how much you are willing to lose ahead of time before you enter the trade. It is being very clear about one thing: if the trade does not work out according to my plan, I will be able to emotionally and financially survive without that loss affecting my life and my financial security.

Market Traders Institute's broker of choice is I-TradeFX (www.itradefx. com). They have an extremely user-friendly trading platform and will instruct you in how to place your protective stop-loss order every time you trade.

Protecting yourself at all times, and in every trade, needs to become a subconscious habit. Never trade without looking at the downside first. Never trade without saying, "If this trade does not work out, can I afford to lose x amount of money?" Protect yourself at all times, and if you take a financial loss, do not take it personally. Trading without protective stop-loss orders is outright exposure to financial self-destruction.

As you learn to trade and gain some experience and taste some success, you step into an arena of false security. That is why people drown in the ocean. They swim with insufficient respect for and knowledge about the ocean—a false sense of security, a feeling that they are greater than the force of the ocean—and they drown. What is amazing is that when someone drowns in the ocean, the ocean meant no harm. It was just doing what it does . . . it just exists.

Like the ocean, the market exists with no feeling, and without the proper knowledge and respect for the market, you, too, can drown financially, and if you do, the market will feel nothing. "Fear always springs from ignorance."

Trading without a protective stop-loss order ignores the potential damage the market can do to you psychologically, emotionally, and financially. If you enter the market without protection and trade without a protective stop-loss order, you are the perfect candidate for a major catastrophic, life-altering event in your trading career. Events that move the market 500 pips in a direction don't happen every day, but surprise fundamental announcements happen all the time.

You must never forget the greatest discovery of experienced traders was that "Murphy" lives in the market. As a matter of fact, he lives in your computer and, when you trade, believe me, "if something can go wrong, it will go wrong." What usually happens is that the first few times you trade without a protective stop-loss order, the market goes a little beyond where you would have placed it, bounces, and then returns to make you whole, and you walk away with a profit. Congratulations, you just ran your first red light without an accident. Like any driver or trader, that is one of the worst things that can happen to you, because you now have acquired that false sense of ability and confidence. As a trader, your subconscious mind recorded the event in detail and is ready to replay one of the biggest lies of a trading career: "The market always comes back. Don't worry, next time you run that red light at 60 miles an hour, just look both ways and you will be alright." Trust me, it will only be a matter of time before you get hit and suffer major consequences.

Scientists say it only takes three repetitions to form a habit. If you trade two or three times with a mental protective stop-loss order or even without one, you will feel you know the market better than the market knows itself. With pride, you will start to feel that you have now harnessed the market and figured out how it moves. You will start to feel happy, confident, and proud of your new trading breakthrough. A costly mistake most traders make is that they enter the market and instead of placing an actual protective stop-loss order with the computer, they feel confident to rely on their "mental" stop-loss order to protect them in the market.

Congratulations, you have just formed a new self-destructive habit. Why? You have just fooled yourself into believing that if the market gets to your mental stop-loss order, you will have the discipline and courage to get out. Well, I am here to tell you, if you trade without a presubmitted or pre-executed protective stop-loss order at the time of entry, it will only be a matter of time before you get caught off-guard. The only way you avoid danger in the market is to properly understand what the market is capable of doing to you.

The Forex can liquidate you in less than five hours. How do I know that? Personal experience. Every trade involves risk. Risk is a part of our lives. We drive defensively and wear seat belts to minimize our risk as we drive. Traders learn where to place their protective stop-loss orders to minimize risk.

Should you choose to drive without a seat belt, don't be surprised if you end up in the hospital after you get hit, and if you trade without a stop-loss order, don't be surprised if you experience the following.

Excited about your newfound profession, trading at home, making money 24 hours a day at your convenience, you enter a trade buying after you did all your homework, and you are proud to be a bull going long in the market. You choose to place a mental stop-loss order for this trade, and to your surprise the market blows by your mental protective stop-loss order. If you do not have the courage to pull the trigger and get out now, then get prepared for the first wild ride in your trading career.

As the market continues running in the opposite direction of your entry, you find yourself now 75 pips in the red. That is $750 in potential losses. You now know you are a little more exposed than you would prefer to be, but you feel confident that bulls will show up and return the market back to your point of entry. The market continues to dip and you are now 100 pips, or $1,000, in the red, and you ask, "Were did all these bears come from? You verbally commit to yourself saying, "If it goes 10 more pips against me, I am out of here. I will have the courage to get out of the market and take the $1,100 dollar loss." All of a sudden bears show up in packs and the market begins to race down droping 50 more pips in four minutes. It is now 150 pips, or $1,500, against you and your courage is now gone. Fear sets in as the market keeps dropping. You are now 200 pips, or $2,000, in the red. Your heart is pounding so fast you can hardly breathe. Things are now very serious, and overwhelming, helpless fear overtakes your being.

Then *boom*, out of the blue, as if someone just refueled the market to keep it going, the market drops another 100 pips and now you are 300 pips in the red, or $3,000 down. You only have $4,000 in your trading account. You told your wife, your family, and your fiends you were embarking on one of the most exiting journeys of your life. And you were right, because things are now pretty exciting!

You have no idea what is going on or what took place in the market to create such a bearish move in the opposite direction from your entry. All you can think about now is survival. You are in shock. You can't believe this is happening to you. I have learned being frightened is an experience you can't buy. A good scare is worth more to a person than good advice.

You sit in silence, looking at your trading screen in true disbelief. As time passes, the market calms down. You feel stalked by the bears while they linger as if they have been hunting you down waiting for you to succumb to satisfy their appetite.

The reality is, your pain is self-inflicted. You are in this state because you either thought you were above the law, or you underestimated the power of the market. Either way, you should have placed a predetermined stop-loss order and been out of the market with a $300 to $500 loss. But no, you were too smart and too courageous for that.

More bears appear, and the market continues to move against you. You feel the bears are slowly devouring every last dollar in your margin trading account. You are now just a few pips away from being completely liqui-dated and eaten alive by those ruthless bears. Suddenly out of nowhere, a beautiful morning star appears on your screen and the market begins to rally in your direction. You yell out, "Yes, somebody has listened to my prayers."

You kiss the screen of your computer as you fall to your knees—you are so excited. You start following that morning star and even though you are still 300 pips, or $3,000, in the red, you now have hope. That hope slowly begins to overcome your feelings of fear, and as the market slowly moves up, your fear begins to dissipate.

You are so relieved and grateful that your cries of help had been answered. You now honor your new commitment to never trade again with-out a protective stop-loss order and you place a protective stop-loss order 10 pips below the low of the morning star and quantify your threshold of pain. In doing that, you have now quantified the worst thing that can hap-pen to you—losing on a trade. With conviction and commitment you say, "If more bears show up and it falls any more, I am going to have to face the music, wake up, and end this nightmare."

You are filled with all these positive feelings of freedom, and the mar-ket drops and tests that morning star. You wonder what's going on. Then *boom*, a huge bullish engulfing candle appears and the market begins to rally. As the market slowly starts to rally and come back in your favor, you walk outside and breathe in fresh air to rekindle your senses. But then, as you go back into the house and look at the charts, you discover that the mar-ket began to wave back down against you. Your emotions and brain are so fried and you are so exhausted you can't even think or recall what you have been taught—that the market waves in a natural up A, B, C, D price move-ment as it climbs.

The reason I can describe this process in such detail is that I have been there, done that, and can warn you about the experience.

Setbacks and failures are a part of life. What you don't want is a setback so devastating that it changes your life forever. When it is time to execute a trade, you can never really quantify how much you can make in a trade; however, you can always quantify how much you are willing to risk, or lose, should the trade not go your way.

The rule of survival at trading is to never risk more than 5 percent of your equity on any given trade. MTI's trading methodologies and strategies teach you how to find excellent trades in the market by risking no more than 50 to 60 pips on any given trade. If you want to be a bull and go long, you will need to place your protective stop-loss orders a little beyond the last low of a major level of support. If you want to be a bear and go short, you will need to place your protective stop-loss order a little beyond the last high or major level of resistance. Most successful money managers make it a habit to risk only 0.5 to 2 percent of your available trading equity on any single trade. The fact is, no one can tell you how much you should risk on a trade, but I will share with you a formula to protect your equity or your trading account.

THE EQUITY MANAGEMENT FORMULA

Most trades will require a 30–50 pip stop-loss order, due to the fact that the market waves constantly, and we need to stay out of the way of the wave. On a $100,000 regular trading account, that equates to between $300–$500 required stop-loss needed to enter that trade. On a $1,000 mini account that equates to between $30–$50 needed to enter the same trade. Always use the Equity Management Formula as displayed in Figure 12-1 to calculate your percentage risk per trade. For example, if you have a balance of $1,000 in your $100,000 regular trading account margin and you need $500 (a 50-pip stop-loss order), then you will risk 50 percent of your entire trading account margin in one single trade. This could financially be disastrous. You always need to strive to remain below 5 percent risk in any trade. In order to stay within the guidelines of effective equity management, you

FIGURE 12-1   Risk Management of Capital

All Trades Have Risk

$100,000 Account

In Margin	$1,000	$2,500	$5,000	$10,000	$15,000
Risk 50 pips	$500	$500	$500	$500	$500
% Risk to Margin	50%	20%	10%	5%	3%

$10,000 Account

In Margin	$1,000	$2,500	$5,000	$10,000	$15,000
Risk 50 pips	$50	$50	$50	$50	$50
% Risk to Margin	5%	2%	1%	0.05%	0.03%

Learn to trade and make your mistakes on a $10,000 account,
after you learn a successful technique,
trade and take profits on a $100,000 account,

will need a minimum balance of between $10,000 to $15,000 to open a $100,000 regular trading account. If you do not have $15,000, you may want to start out with a mini account where you need at least $1,000 to open a $1,000 mini trading account. Traders have the luxury of determining their risk before they enter the market.

Do not only stay focused on the potential gain. You need to stay focused on the potential risk when making any trade. If you cannot afford the risk, do not trade! Whatever you do, never overtrade your account and place yourself at financial risk.

Financial survival is critical. If your dream is to become a successful trader, you cannot run out of money before you accomplish your dream or the dream is over. Do not overtrade your account. The reason you need to risk only a certain percentage of your trading margin is so that you have staying power in the market. Figure 12-2 points out that the more money you start out with, and the lower the amount you risk, the more staying power you will have in the market.

Remember, there is no such thing as the "trade of the century" or a "sure thing" when it comes to trading. Do not move from one lot to five lots if your equity management is not in line with this. If you do, you will lose on the five-lot trade, incur an emotional scar, and you will be back down to trading with single lots again on your trades to follow. Your margin account will take a big financial hit, and it will now take you five times as long to make up that loss. Regardless of how good a trade looks, you must maintain the discipline to trade within the rules of equity management.

FIGURE 12-2   Understanding the Term *Over-Trading*

Do Not Overtrade Your 100K Account

Overtrading

In Margin	$1,000	$2,500	$5,000	$10,000	$15,000
Risk 50 pips	$500	$500	$500	$500	$500
% Risk to Margin	50%	20%	10%	5%	3%
No. of losses you canendure	1	4	9	19	29

Copyright 2005 by Market Traders Institute, Inc.

RISK VERSUS REWARD

There is no need to ever sell the farm for any given trade. When a trader says, "Here comes the big one. I feel it!" and tells their spouse or significant other, "Let us risk everything because this one is going to pay off," rest assured, it will be the one to take you down. The risk must, at minimum, equal the reward and, in most cases, must be far less than the reward. The rule for the risk versus reward must be a minimum of 1:1. I say minimum because your habit of success must be 1:1.5. In other words, for every dollar you risk, you must plan to make 1.5 times the return. When you risk $500, your projected gain must consistently be $750.

Market participants that are long-term traders, like banks and large financial institutions, will risk more on their trades, but their trades still equate to 1 to 2 percent of their equity, and their targets for gain will be in alignment with the 1 to 1.5 risk versus reward ratio.

PERCENTAGES MEAN NOTHING WHEN TRADING

Great traders are only right 50 to 60 percent of the time. They make lots of money because they keep their losses small and gains big. If I said I was a good trader, but I lost 70 percent of the time, would you give me your money to trade? Percentages mean nothing in trading.

For example, you can be wrong 70 percent of the time and still make lots of money:

Seven losses out of 10 at $400 apiece is $2,800.00.
Three gains at $1,500 apiece equals $4,500 in profit.
Subtract the losses from the gains and you have a net gain of $1,700
    being wrong 70 percent of the time.

Look what happens to your profit if you are able to trade with smaller losses and larger profits (see Figure 12-3).

When greed exceeds your need, it will usually take you down a path of self-destruction.

You know what has always amazed me is that when the average couple's refrigerator breaks, the first thing they do is immediately get a cooler to save the food. If they don't have one, they will go out and buy one. Then they will take the leftover, unmelted ice and dump it in the cooler. If there is not enough ice, they will go out and buy some. After they calm down from the frustration of the refrigerator breaking, over the next seven days, they will

FIGURE 12-3   Winning and Losing Percentages

Percentages Mean Nothing...
Can you be a 30% winner and
70% loser and still make money?

No. of Wins	3 or 30% X $2,000 gain per trade =	$6,000
No. of Losses	7 or 70% X $300 loss per trade =	$2,100
	Net Profit =	$3,900

Focus on your losses
Make sure they are small
Let your profits run
And success will come your way

Copyright 2003 by Market Traders Institute, Inc.

go directly from work every night and not only price a new refrigerator but also will learn everything there is to know about refrigerators. They will learn how many cubic inches it has, how many ice cubes it make per hour, how much electricity it consumes per day, as if any of that really matters. All any of us need is place to keep food cold. Period. At the end of seven days of intense research, the husband and wife sit down and have one of the deepest conversations they have had in three years over which model they should buy. Just as a decision is about to be made, one of them will say, "Let's sleep on it one more night before we make this major $995 decision."

Sound familiar? Now watch what happens when a neighbor comes over and says, "You've got to get involved with this deal. I just heard about a hot tip from a stock clerk at work. He told me a $5,000 investment in this deal will bring $50,000 inside of 90 days." Before you know it, you are handing over $5,000 within 24 hours to a broker, so you can become broker.

Think about it. You research everything there is to possibly know about a refrigerator, a necessary and tangible asset in your life that is only going to cost $1,000, yet your neighbor, who is dumber than you are, comes over and tells you about this great inside tip he heard about from a stock clerk, who is dumber than the two of you, and you immediately scramble to find as much money as you can to invest. If you had $10,000, you would invest it. As a matter of fact, the very next morning when you call your broker to invest, you tell him you only can invest $5,327, because that is everything you have, and you continue talking in an apologetic tone telling him you wish you had more to invest.

At the end of 90 days, guess what? Surprise! You are not rich! As a matter of fact, you are $5,327 poorer.

Financially successful people have learned to educate themselves about any opportunity before they get involved or they don't get involved at all.

As they do their due diligence, they educate themselves about the opportunity in detail, because when you find out as much as you can about something, it gives you options. Their number one focus is to determine how much they could lose if this opportunity does not work out. They quantify a potential loss before they get involved. They attach a dollar amount to it and a deadline to the opportunity, and whichever one is hit first, they are disciplined enough to get out and walk away. They refuse to attach their emotions or self-worth to any opportunity. When their idea or opportunity does not work, they don't keep going deeper and deeper in the red. They get out and move on.

Savvy investors have one major focus: the preservation of their initial capital. They already know the price they had to pay to get that money. They are not driven by greed, and they don't want to re-earn the principal again. They first look at risk, then the consequences of taxes, and, lastly, the potential of returns.

Poor investors are people with limited funds for a reason. They look first at return and say, "I am not worried about the taxes, after all, when this opportunity pays off, and it will, I will have plenty of money for taxes." They look at preservation of capital and their risk factor last. That is why they are poor.

CONCLUSION

A trader's journey can and needs to be fun, and losses need to be avoided at all cost. A 300-pip, or $3,000, potential loss is not a prosperous, happy event to experience. It is terrifying. If you hate trading with tight stops, trade with larger ones, but, whatever you do, protect yourself at all times.

Here is what you need to understand as you move forward in trading. You will be introduced to emotions in a way you never thought possible.

As you trade and incur losses along the way, you must remember, the absolute worst thing that could happen to you is that you will lose all the money in your trading account. Allow me to put that into perspective for you.

As you trade, no one is going to kill you or your family. The mean tax man is not going to come and take away everything you own. You won't lose your house or your car as you trade. No one is going to expose your deepest and darkest secret. The worst thing that can happen to you is you lose your money in your margin account and your ego gets bruised from not being right in the trade. That's it.

If you can put this into perspective as you continue to learn how to trade, you will be well on your way to becoming a successful trader.

The next time you pull the trigger to trade, ask yourself, "Can I afford to take the loss?" If the answer is no, then don't trade. It is that simple. If the answer is yes, enter the trade and move forward hoping for the best and preparing for the worst, and the worst thing that can happen is your stop-loss order gets hit and you take a predetermined loss (that you were willing to risk).

Create a disaster plan before you get involved with anything. That way, when disaster strikes, it is not a disaster, it was merely part of the plan. Anticipate your future challenges and potential problems. In thinking through what might, and can, happen, you save yourself from having to deal with the problem in an emotional state of fear. Get rid of your fear before you trade. If, by chance, life or the market surprises you with something you were not expecting, calm down and start to think through the problem logically. In the past, when you were faced with a problem and you were fearful, it was because you didn't have or see the answer or solution to your problem. Fear only goes away when you have a solution. You avoid fear in the market by quantifying a protective stop and trading with a stop-loss order.

We get involved in trading because it is exciting and holds the promise of financial success. We also see it as a way to make money on our terms, trading from home, not having a boss, no employees, no inventory or receivables, no headaches, making money 24 hours a day at our convenience. Then, *whack*, you take your first loss, and the money is gone right out of your account.

You say, "No problem, they told me about this." Then, *whack*, another loss, and more money is gone. Now you become a little concerned. Then, *whack*, another loss, and even more money is gone. Market losses are quick and non-negotiable. You see all this money gone and you are scared and fearful. Your judgment is challenged. Your ego is challenged. Your common sense is challenged. More importantly, everyone you told about this is watching you and expecting a favorable report. What are you going to do?

Don't fear the market—respect it. It is not to be feared, it is only to be understood. You will not become a good trader if plagued with fear. You have to face that fear head-on with all the courage in the world, as the only difference between hero and a coward is how they respond in time of fear. Both are scared to death; however, the coward cowers down and runs the other way, whereas the hero faces his fear, attacks it head-on, and triumphs over it.

13

THE FINAL
ANALYSIS

I REALLY ENJOYED WRITING this book and hope you have enjoyed reading it. I have read a lot of technical books on trading, and most of them have been extremely boring and hard to understand, so I've tried hard to make this one more entertaining.

We have an office in Derry, Ireland, and a dear friend of mine, Kevin McGowan, owns it. He has been a real blessing in my life and has taught me a lot, starting soon after we first met. As I was getting ready to teach him what I knew about the Forex, he pulled me aside and said, "Chief, as you move forward teaching me about the Forex, explain it to me as if I were a 2-year-old and then I will understand." Since then, I have thought of that statement every time I have attempted to explain something to someone.

I want to end this book with a dramatic battle between the bulls and the bears. It is a battle where the bulls seek to destroy the bears, marching out of the wilderness by night catching the bears off-guard as they lie in hibernation, slaying every bear in their sight in an attempt to finally end the ongoing war between the bulls and the bears. To their surprise, the tables turn. The bulls underestimated the strength and endurance of the bears, and the bears once again rise in the fullness of their wrath, forcing the bulls to flee for safety back into bull country to regroup. However, this time, a clear sentiment is surfacing in each respective camp. The next battle will need to be fought with the determination and commitment of total annihilation; a final battle that frees the world of any and all future conflict; a battle that finally brings peace to the land.

Each respective camp prepares for war, the bulls charge once again hoping to catch the bears off-guard only to find them well prepared and ready for battle. So great and lasting becomes this war that there is no time to bury the dead. There is only time to fight and survive. A battle that completely and utterly destroys two nations committed to their causes and beliefs. In the end they all fall by the sword, leaving only two surviving warriors, an exhausted bull and an exhausted bear, perhaps, the nations' leaders or generals, standing eye-to-eye.

As they gaze into each others eyes and at their surroundings, they both finally realize they are the only two standing and that they are both covered with massive battle wounds. The realization that millions of bulls and bears including all their loved ones and their personal possessions have been destroyed is beyond their mortal comprehension. Barely able to stand, they contemplate what their opponents' next move might be and their minds begin to wonder:

- Was their cause just?

- Was it even worth it?

As they stand there filled with pain, the bull begins to remember the words of his father "that in life, you either control your own destiny or someone else will!"

Resting on his sword, the bear is caught off-guard as the bull charges one last time, cutting off the head of the bear. With the decapitated bear's head on the ground, the bear's body stands on its two hind legs, claws extended and begins to charge as if it just found new energy to attack one last time ... struggling as it steps forward, the bears body takes one last breath, then falls to the ground and dies. Standing in shock and disbelief of what just took place, the bull collapses from sheer exhaustion. Lying there lifeless and filled with sorrow, the bull concludes there is no reason to live. These words begin to resonate from the bull: "Life is clearly about suffering, and happiness only comes to those who can find meaning in the suffering."

With no ability to find any meaning at everything that just happened, the bull takes his last breath and dies of a broken spirit, leaving all their bodies to become prey for the other beasts of the world.

In the end, if this were the course of events, I would then want to analyze what happened. Why it was that the war had to be an all-or-nothing war? Why couldn't there have been a compromise? What exactly was it that drove them to such madness, such hatred, and eventual self-destruction? But I can't because the war continues and will continue.

You see, the world is round and is a place where there is no beginning and there is no end, only a continuation; an infinite marathon where the baton is passed from one generation to another. What might seem like an ending to some becomes the beginning to others. Either way, life needs to be about progression not regression.

Trading has changed my life.

I am who I am because of what I have seen, heard, and experienced. Good and bad. We are all a compilation of everything we have seen, heard, and experienced. I am grateful for everything I have been able to experience, including all the negative. I don't think I would have amounted to much if it weren't for the adversity in my life. I have learned that adversity is the blow or strike that sharpens the sword.

As you learn to trade on the Forex, or any market for that matter, put it all into perspective. Make sure trading is a part of your life and not your entire life. Make sure you are able to digest your food and sleep at night when you are in a long-term trading position. Sure, there is no success without sacrifice, but never forget the market moves on its own time frame, not yours. As it moves on its time frame, be disciplined and control your desire for instant gratification, because it is only the delayed gratification that will bring you long-term success.

I hope you realize that there really is no true secret to success. It is for you, it is for me, it is for everyone. If there was a secret to success, it would be to straighten out what is between our ears. Ignorance has its price. In reality, success is achieved in inches, not in miles.

My grandson, Jeffery, came home from school one day and said, "I know why you are so rich, Grandpa!"

I said, "Why?" (Remember, wealth is relative at his age: $1,000 is all the money in the world.)

He said, "I learned today from a guest speaker in school that most poor people read one book every 5 to 10 years. Average income earners read one book every 3 to 5 years, but rich people read at least one book a month." He looked at my bookshelf, filled with hundreds of books, and asked, "Which book do you want me to read, Grandpa?" I smiled at him and handed him a book titled *Children the Challenge*.

Obviously, his guest speaker read the same article I did. The article goes on to describe how a university conducted a study on the daily habits of low-, average-, and high-income earners. To their surprise, they discovered that low-income earners read on average one book every 10 years. Average-income earners read a book, on average, once every five years. But, not surprisingly, they found that high-income earners read, on average, one book every month, and that book often has to do with either their current profession or self-improvement. Pretty amazing, and I would say fairly accurate, as I have read well over 500 books in my life, half on self-improvement. How many books have you read in the past year? What were they about? "Education has its reward, and ignorance has its price."

USA Today, America's largest newspaper, did a study and was able to prove this statement: education has its reward, and ignorance has its price. Look at their findings:

Average Salary by Education Level

No high school	$16,053 per year
High school graduate	$23,594 per year
Some college	$27,566 per year
Bachelor's degree	$43,782 per year
Advanced degree	$63,473 per year

Think about it as you look at the above facts. The difference between dropping out of high school versus finishing what you started and receiving a diploma equates with an average of $7,541 more per year in income.

If you are going to learn how to trade on the Forex and don't take the time to educate yourself first or be guided by a mentor trader who is already successful, you will probably lose all the money you start with.

If you say, "I cannot afford to take the time to educate myself before I trade," remember, "ignorance has its price." If you are one of the people who say, "I would rather take any money I would spend on education and put it into my live trading account, giving me more money to trade with," then *don't trade*. If you do, you will pay the price in trading losses. Remember: "Experience is what you get, when you don't get what you want." In trading, you need experience and education.

Our company talks to people every day from around the world, many of whom say, "I can't afford the price of education." Our only response is, "You can't afford not to educate yourself."

EDUCATION FIRST

Before you begin trading on the Forex, you need to know:

1. How to make money
2. How to protect yourself financially

The only difference between successful traders and unsuccessful traders is that the unsuccessful ones don't know what they are doing and keep losing more money in a desperate attempt to get it all back. They are no different than all the gamblers who go to casinos.

Successful traders know exactly what happens when they lose money and know how to put the losses into perspective. They don't desperately chase the market, trying to make up for past losses. They don't waste any time dwelling on the past, rather, they stay focused on what future trading opportunities exist—and that is what makes them successful.

OUR HABITS CONTROL OUR LIVES

In Chapter 1, I talked about how important it is to establish a solid moral and ethical constitution in our lives and the value of having a solid work ethic. Don't forget, who and what you are is what you will bring to the trading table. You will bring all your good habits and all your bad habits alike. All your good habits will enhance your trading, but all your bad habits will be magnified and most certainly intensify as you trade and could potentially destroy you.

I pointed out that we are not what we think we are. We are not what we tell other people we are. We are not what we verbally promise to other people. We are what we do. What we do is who we are. Our actions are our automatic habits. Those habits force us in a position to either manage our daily poverty, daily mediocrity, or daily success.

Learning to become a successful currency trader is a dream of thousands of people around the world. Let me assure you, it is a worthy goal. I have learned that every dream is in the mind of the believer and in the hands of the doer. We are not given dreams without being given the power to make them come true.

If you are not making the money in your life you always dreamed of, perhaps it is because you are locked into a series of unproductive work habits or a self-destructive mindset. Perhaps you have created a mental block that has stopped you from earning more than you think you are worth. If you want to earn more than you are earning right now, you must upgrade your self-concept. Hopefully, this book can get you started in upgrading your self-concept. Always remember: "If another person can do it, you can do it."

FINDING YOUR POT OF GOLD

Learning to trade on the Forex is your new rainbow. Your greater pot of gold at the end of this rainbow surprisingly will have nothing to do with money, it will be who you become as you slowly purge yourself of all your self-destructive habits that have stood in the way of earning more than you thought you were worth. Remember in life, it is not about what you acquire that counts, it is what you become!

As you trade on the Forex, you will have a choice to make: conquer or crumble. If you choose to conquer and persist until you succeed, you will become a totally different person. Your new productive habits will have an impact not only in your work life but also in your home, family, and personal life.

No journey is complete, however, without surprises and complications. Frustrations and even bad things will happen along the way. You will, no doubt, incur some "trading scars."

Your mistakes, setbacks, and failures will not only create disappointment, they will also place you in a pressure cooker of performance. Do not fear the pressure—embrace it. Remember that if there is no pressure, there are no diamonds. Life keeps striking only those who are prepared to become that perfect diamond. Be grateful for every blunt strike that comes your way. There is nothing wrong with getting rid of the rough edges in your life, which is really getting rid of your bad habits.

You will need to master the art of forgetting, forgiving, and moving on. Remember that the reason the windshield on your car is 50 times larger than the rearview mirror is because we are to stay focused on where we are going in our journey and not where we have been. You cannot waste time dwelling on the past. The market is constantly on the move, creating new opportunities for those traders prepared to take advantage of them. You must stay focused on those new opportunities, learn from your mistakes, and move on.

Don't ever forget that the most valuable things in life cannot be bought with money. You cannot buy love, you cannot buy loyalty, you cannot buy respect, and you most certainly cannot buy time.

I often wondered what experiences Mother Theresa went through as she dedicated her time serving the world that allowed her to write "The Final Analysis". Her final analysis changed *everything*.

"The Final Analysis," by Mother Theresa

People are often unreasonable, illogical and self centered ... forgive them anyway!

If you are kind, people may accuse you of selfish, ulterior motives ... be kind anyway!

If you are successful, you will win some false friends
and make some true enemies ... succeed anyway!

if you are honest and frank, people may cheat you,
... be honest and frank anyway

What you spend years building, someone may destroy
overnight ... go ahead and build it anyway!

If you find serenity and happiness, people may be
jealous ... be happy anyway!

the good you do today, people will often forget
tomorrow ... do good anyway!

Give the world the best you have, and even that may
never be enough ... give it anyway!

You see in the final analysis, its all between you and God,
it was never between you and them anyway!!

The experiences in my life have led me to write my "final analysis on trading": "When it comes time to trade, it is between you and your bad habits ... it was never meant to be between the bulls and the bears anyway!"

Health, Happiness, and Successful Trading

GLOSSARY

Ask Rate The rate at which a financial instrument if offered for sale (as in bid/ask spread).

Base Currency In general terms, the base currency is the currency in which an investor or issuer maintains its book of accounts. In the FX markets, the US Dollar is normally considered the "base" currency for quotes, meaning that quotes are expressed as a unit of $1 USD per the other currency quoted in the pair. The primary exceptions to this rule are the British Pound, the Euro and the Australian Dollar.

Bear Market A market distinguished by declining prices.

Bid/Ask Spread The difference between the bid and offer price, and the most widely used measure of market liquidity.

Broker An individual or firm that acts as an intermediary, putting together buyers and sellers for a fee or commission. In contrast, a 'dealer' commits capital and takes one side of a position, hoping to earn a spread (profit) by closing out the position in a subsequent trade with another party.

Bretton Woods Agreement of 1944 An agreement that established fixed foreign exchange rates for major currencies, provided for central bank intervention in the currency markets, and pegged the price of gold at US $35 per ounce. The agreement lasted until 1971, when President Nixon overturned the Bretton Woods agreement and established a floating exchange rate for the major currencies.

Bull Market A market distinguished by rising prices.

Candlestick Chart   A chart that indicates the trading range for the day as well as the opening and closing price. If the open price is higher than the close price, the rectangle between the open and close price is shaded. If the close price is higher than the open price, that area of the chart is not shaded.

Clearing   The process of settling a trade.

Commission   A transaction fee charged by a broker.

Currency   Any form of money issued by a government or central bank and used as legal tender and a basis for trade.

Currency Risk   The probability of an adverse change in exchange rates.

Day Trading   Refers to positions which are opened and closed on the same trading day.

Dealer   An individual who acts as a principal or counterpart to a transaction. Principals take one side of a position, hoping to earn a spread (profit) by closing out the position in a subsequent trade with another party. In contrast, a broker is an individual or firm that acts as an intermediary, putting together buyers and sellers for a fee or commission.

Economic Indicator   A government issued statistic that indicates current economic growth and stability. Common indicators include employment rates, Gross Domestic Product (GDP), inflation, retail sales, etc.

EURO   The currency of the European Monetary Union (EMU). A replacement for the European Currency Unit (ECU).

Federal Reserve (Fed)   The Central Bank for the United States.

Foreign Exchange   (Forex, FX)   The simultaneous buying of one currency and selling of another.

Fundamental analysis   Analysis of economic and political information with the objective of determining future movements in a financial market.

Good 'Til Cancelled Order (GTC)   An order to buy or sell at a specified price. This order remains open until filled or until the client cancels.

Initial margin   The initial deposit of collateral required to enter into a position as a guarantee on future performance.

Interbank rates   The Foreign Exchange rates at which large international banks quote other large international banks.

Limit order   An order with restrictions on the maximum price to be paid or the minimum price to be received. As an example, if the current price of USD/YEN is 102.00/05, then a limit order to buy USD would be at a price below 102. (i.e., 101.50)

Liquidity The ability of a market to accept large transactions with minimal to no impact on price stability.

Liquidation The closing of an existing position through the execution of an offsetting transaction.

Long position A position that appreciates in value if market prices increase.

Margin call A request from a broker or dealer for additional funds or other collateral to guarantee performance on a position that has moved against the customer.

Market Risk Exposure to changes in market prices.

Mark-to-Market Process of reevaluating all open positions with the current market prices. These new values then determine margin requirements.

Offer The rate at which a dealer is willing to sell a currency.

One Cancels the Other Order (OCO) A designation for two orders whereby one part of the two orders is executed the other is automatically cancelled.

Open order An order that will be executed when a market moves to its designated price. Normally associated with Good 'til Cancelled Orders.

Open position A deal not yet reversed or settled with a physical payment.

Over the Counter (OTC) Used to describe any transaction that is not conducted over an exchange.

Overnight A trade that remains open until the next business day.

Pips Digits added to or subtracted from the fourth decimal place, i.e. 0.0001. Also called Points.

Position The netted total holdings of a given currency.

Quote An indicative market price, normally used for information purposes only.

Rate The price of one currency in terms of another, typically used for dealing purposes.

Resistance A term used in technical analysis indicating a specific price level at which analysis concludes people will sell.

Risk Exposure to uncertain change, most often used with a negative connotation of adverse change.

Risk Management The employment of financial analysis and trading techniques to reduce and/or control exposure to various types of risk.

Roll-Over   Process whereby the settlement of a deal is rolled forward to another value date. The cost of this process is based on the interest rate differential of the two currencies.

Settlement   The process by which a trade is entered into the books and records of the counterparts to a transaction. The settlement of currency trades may or may not involve the actual physical exchange of one currency for another.

Short Position   An investment position that benefits from a decline in market price.

Spot Price   The current market price. Settlement of spot transactions usually occurs within two business days.

Spread   The difference between the bid and offer prices.

Sterling   Slang for British Pound.

Stop Loss Order   Order type whereby an open position is automatically liquidated at a specific price. Often used to minimize exposure to losses if the market moves against an investor's position. As an example, if an investor is long USD at 156.27, they might wish to put in a stop loss order for 155.49, which would limit losses should the dollar depreciate, possibly below 155.49.

Support Levels   A technique used in technical analysis that indicates a specific price ceiling and floor at which a given exchange rate will automatically correct itself. Opposite of resistance.

Technical Analysis   An effort to forecast prices by analyzing market data, i.e. historical price trends and averages, volumes, open interest, etc.

Transaction Cost   The cost of buying or selling a financial instrument.

Transaction Date   The date on which a trade occurs.

US Prime Rate   The interest rate at which US banks will lend to their prime corporate customers

Index

A

Accumulation, 175–186
Asian Forex markets
    financial problems of, 21

B

Bankruptcy, 91
Bear(s)
    and bulls, 25
    scoring points with, 74
    timing of bullish positions, 94
    traps, 185
Bearish candlestick formations, 111, 179
    future resistance, 84
    near resistance, 83
    reversal patterns, 62–68
Bearish engulfing candle, 65–66
Bearish engulfing lines, 54
Bearish engulfing pattern, 64
    investor psychology behind, 64–65
Bracketing, 168, 175–186
Bretton-Woods Accord, 19–20
Bull(s)
    and bear, 25
    dealing with downtrends, 82–83
    price location support at, 80

resistance locations of, 82
scoring points with, 74
timing of bearish positions, 94
traps, 184–186
Bullen, David, 72
Bullish candlestick formations, 57,
    81–83, 111
Bullish engulfing candle, 59
Bullish engulfing line, 53
Bullish engulfing patterns
    investor psychology of, 60
    signal, 59
Buy zones, 113–127
    bullish candle entrance of, 122
    definition, 117
    differences of, 122
    going long during, 126
    market entrance of, 123
    trend line division of, 117

C

Candlestick formations, 56–57, 180. *See
    also* Japanese candlestick
    bearish, 62–68, 83, 84, 111, 179
    bullish, 57, 81–83, 111
Capital preservation, 197

CCI. *See* Consumer Confidence
    Index (CCI)
Challenger, 89
Character analysis, 4
Chicago Mercantile Exchange (CME), 48
CME. *See* Chicago Mercantile
    Exchange (CME)
Commitments
    importance of keeping them, 5
Consolidation
    factors, 175–186
    trading range of, 181
Constitution-based *versus*
    feeling-based, 14
Constructive ego, 11
Consumer Confidence Index (CCI), 172
Consumer Price Index (CPI), 172
Convergence, 80
CPI. *See* Consumer Price Index (CPI)
Currency markets
    Forex trading with, 164
Currency trading
    differences of, 90

D

Dark cloud cover, 54
Destructive ego, 11
Devaluation, 21
Doji, 55
    double, 55
    dragonfly, 54
    gravestone, 55
    long legged, 54
    star, 54
Dow Jones Industrial
    chart of September 11, 2001, 154
Downtrend lines
    drawing of, 105
    incorrect ways of, 107–108
    long-term, 106–107
    market break of, 123
    market support of, 110
Downtrends, 141
    channel shifts, 125
    lines of, 105, 111
    numerical sequences of, 141
    steps to be followed for, 149

Dragonfly doji, 54
Durable goods order, 172

E

ECI. *See* Employment Cost Index (ECI)
Emotional reactions and responses, 10
Employment Cost Index (ECI), 164
Equity management
    formula, 193
    rules of, 187–199
Euro
    introduction of, 21
European monetary system, 20–21
Evening star, 54, 62
    formations, 63
    investor psychology behind, 64
Existing home sales, 173
Exit strategies, 41–43

F

Federal Reserve Bank, 165
Feeling-based *versus* constitution-based, 14
Fibonacci
    history of, 131–132
    knowledge of, 129, 149
Fibonacci, Leonardo, 129
    mathematical concepts developed
        by, 131
Fibonacci extension, 148
    in nature, 157–159
    in reference to September 11,
        2001, 152
Fibonacci market movement
    in reference to September 11, 2001,
        151–155
Fibonacci numbers, 45, 130
    ratio, 158
    in reference to market, 147
    sequences, 130, 132, 185
    series, 135
    value of, 146–147
Fibonacci ratios, 135, 150
    composition of human body, 137
    Greek knowledge of, 139
    Pythagoras, 139
    in reference to resistance, 142, 144
    in reference to support, 142, 144

Fibonacci retracement, 156
  and extension ratio relationship, 140–146
  level, 143, 149
  locations at, 155–157
  in nature, 157–159
  in reference to September 11,
    2001, 152
Fibonacci secret, 129–149
  reality of, 151–159
Fibonacci sequence
  areas of our lives existence, 135
  nature of, 132–140
Financial goals
  seminars on, 1
Financial markets
  individual trades of, 72
  with near-perfect Fibonacci
    balance, 153
Fleeing to safety, 163
Foreign exchange market (Forex), 2
  bears, 73
  bulls, 73
  definition of, 21
  education training companies, 33
  history of, 19–21
  independence of, 31
  introduction of, 17–30
  learning to trade, 205
  liquidation of, 191
  self-empowerment of, 31
  successful trading, 15
  traders
    problems with, 43
    types of, 22
  trading, 78, 186, 188
    amount of income, 203
    bearish moves of, 191
    bears, 115–127, 201
    bulls of, 115, 201
    education of, 197, 204–205
    fight for trading, 115
    fundamental announcements of, 163
    getting in, 74
    getting out, 74
    identification of highs, 75
    identification of lows, 75
    mindset of, 3
  shorting of market, 81
  strong currencies used, 19
  transactions in Great Britain, 170
Forex. *See* Foreign exchange market
    (Forex)
Free-floating currencies, 20
Fundamental analysis, 161–174
Fundamental announcements, 162
  consolidation of, 183
  dealing with, 171
  market movements, 182
  trading of, 169, 174

G
Gains
  profits, 43
GDP. *See* Gross Domestic Product (GDP)
Get-rich-quick schemes, 32
Golden ratio, 140
Gold standard, 20
Gravestone doji, 55
Gross Domestic Product (GDP), 164, 173

H
Habits of action, 7
Hammer, 53
Harami, 55
Home sales
  existing, 173
Homma, Munehisa, 48

I
IMF. *See* International Monetary
    Fund (IMF)
Income
  by education level, 204
Indicators
  abundance of, 44
Inner downtrend lines
  finding of, 106–107
Inner trend line
  projected bounce of, 101
Inner uptrend lines
  finding of, 98–99
  hourly charts of, 99
International Monetary Fund (IMF), 19
International trade, 174

Iraq
American declaration of war, 163
iTradeFX, 189

J
Japanese candlestick
chart reading, 50
formations, 179
history of, 47–49
how to read, 49
market highs, 51
market lows, 51
reading, 50
trading of, 47–70
understanding different number
of, 52–55

L
Leverage, 23–25
Liber Abaci, 132
Light, 168
Limit order, 26
Litmus test, 4
Long legged doji, 54
Long-term downtrend lines
finding of, 106–107
Long-term trader
selling signals for, 90
Long-term trading position, 203
Long-term uptrend lines
finding of, 98–99
Losses, 43

M
Margin account
loses, 198
Market
ceilings, 105
consolidation, 40, 178
conspiracies, 154
order, 25
pullbacks, 79
self-fulfillment of, 3
Market direction
trading strategy from all directions, 37
Market reversals, 103, 125, 182
probability factors of determination, 124

Market shifts
of upward trends, 116
Market Traders Institute (MTI), 17
class, 84
4.0 charting program, 33–34
indicators of, 36
market direction of, 35
oscillators of, 36
4.0 trading software, 142
market direction, 39, 42
philosophy, 28
trader's checklist, 30
Trend Scalper, 37
Trend Tracker, 38
Market trading, 188
in downtrend, 105
Money trading, 102
Morning star, 53, 57
formations, 58
investor psychology of, 59
Moving trend line, 35
MTI. *See* Market Traders Institute (MTI)
Munehisa Homma, 48
Murphy's law, 107

N
Negative mindset, 12
Non-farm payroll indicator, 172–173
Numerical sequences. *See also* Fibonacci
numbers; Fibonacci sequence
dealing with pinecones, 134
dealing with rabbits, 133
dealing with sunflowers, 134
in nature, 133
ratios in face, 140
in reference to body ratios, 139
in reference to piano's octaves, 136
in reference to pyramids, 137

O
OCO. *See* One cancels other (OCO)
Off-currencies, 170
One cancels other (OCO)
orders, 27
trading of, 43
Orders
types of, 25–27

Outer downtrend lines
  finding of, 106–107
Outer trend line
  projected bounce of, 101
Outer uptrend lines, 98–99
  hourly charts of, 99

P

Pesavento, Larry, 130
Piercing line, 53
Pips. *See* Price interest points (pips)
Positive mindset, 12
PPI. *See* Producer Price Index (PPI)
Pressure performance, 18
Price interest points (pips), 23
  profit of, 41
  protective stop-loss order of, 192
Producer Price Index (PPI), 173

R

Rainbow chasers, 2
  setting of goals, 14
Reactive bad habits, 10
Reactive trading, 11
Resistance
  definition for, 75–77
  difference in lows, 76–77
  financial game of, 71–87
  finding levels of, 111
Retail sales, 174
Reversal patterns, 57
Rewards *vs.* risks, 195
Risks *vs.* rewards, 195
Roman numeral system, 132

S

Scalpers, 22
Sell zones, 113–127
  definition, 117
  market entrance of, 118
  shorting of market, 121–122
  trend line division of, 117
September 11, 2001
  effect of, 151–155
Shooting star, 54
Shorting market, 81
Sideways movement, 175–186

Slippage, 26
Small trading range, 177
S &P. *See*-Standard and Poors (S&P)
Speculative investor, 21
Speculative trader, 21
Spinning tops, 55
Standard and Poors (S &P)
  chart of September 11, 2001, 155
Star, 55
Stop-loss order, 189
Stop orders, 26
Straddle, 181
Successful people
  influence of mentor, 2
Successful trading
  control of emotions, 9
  following rules, 6
  importance of listening, 6
  setting goals, 14
  steps for, 4
  thinking before you act, 9
  unproductive actions of bad habit, 8
  work through frustration, 28
  worrying about losses, 13
Support
  definition for, 75
  financial game of, 71–87
  finding levels of, 111

T

Teaching concepts, 18
3 percent rule, 29
Traders
  methods for payment, 23
  risk determination of, 194
  success of, 87
  types of, 22–23
Trading, 50
  with bears, 86
  with bulls, 86
  calculated risks of, 87
  candlestick patterns, 68
  common sense during, 127
  consolidation, 186
  critical facets of, 27
  final analysis, 206
  financial success of, 198

indicators, 37
levels of, 28–29
market predictors for, 70
meanings of percentages, 195
negative habits of, 205
personal experiences of, 187
positive habits of, 205
reality of, 29
risk of, 121
scars, 206
as secondary income, 24
straddles, 183
studying market movement for, 146
trending of market, 116
using multiple frames, 44
without stop-loss order, 189
Trading channels, 110
buy zones, 120
with sell zones, 120
trading lines of, 110
Trading days
trending days, 167
Trading fundamental announcements
increased risk with, 167–169
Trading plans
discipline required for, 87
Trading software
via self-empowerment, 31–45
Trading strategies, 178
components of, 34
Trading volume
fundamentals of, 181
Trend(s), 89–111, 115–117
breaking by market, 118
inside of trends, 108–110
time frames of, 94
Trend lines, 89–111
angle of, 119, 123
breaks, 126

computer automation of,
103–104
downtrends of, 95
importance of straight, 103
penetration of, 116
speeds of, 143
uptrends of, 95
value of, 111
Tulip Mania, 48
Tweezer bottom bullish formation,
60–62
Tweezer psychology
behind tweezer bottoms, 62
Tweezer top formation, 66, 67
investor psychology, 66–67
21-day, 3 percent rule, 29

U
Unsuccessful business
emotional decisions, 9
Up swings
different speeds of, 145
Uptrend lines
drawing of, 96–97
incorrect ways of drawing, 100
long-term, 98–99
Uptrends, 141
dealing with market retracement, 146
lines of, 111
numerical sequences of, 141
spotting, 96–97
steps to be followed for, 148

W
Wealth accumulation, 1
Whiplashes, 169
Wicks, 49
World economies, 169–170
World Trade Center, 152

About the Author

JARED F. MARTINEZ is the founder of Market Traders Institute, Inc., the worldwide leader in Forex education with more than 10,000 clients. Martinez is the founder of the I-TradeFX Brokerage Firm and is globally renowned in all trading arenas. He is best known for trading the natural Fibonacci movements in the market that help traders turn patterns into profit. He is also a contributor to "FX Television," *Stocks and Commodities, FX Street*, and *Active Trader*. Martinez has mentored thousands of traders from novices to experts.